SADAAT

SYED SHADAB ALI

Contents

Contents

From The Author -

Beginning with the name of Allah, who is the most beneficent and merciful, who is the first of the first and the last of the last. All praise is only for that one and only Rab, Allah, who created the pure servants full of sanctity like Muhammad, Ali, Fatima and Hasnain Kareemain (Sallal lahu alaihe wa aalihi wa sallam) and who created the fourteen innocents and the Ahlebait, Alaihimussalam.

Every physical and spiritual worship is for only one God.

The Allah who gave us Furqaan al Hameed, The Allah who gave us life, will give us death and will make us alive again. My Allah is Malik-e-Yaumiddin (Lord of the day of Judgement), my Allah is Rab-e-Kaaba (Lord of the holy Kaaba), He is Rab ul Maghribain, he is Rab ul Mashrikain (Lord of Directions)

He is the benevolent; he forgives every sin, every mistake and does justice.

Even when there was nothing anywhere, only He was there.

Even when everything will be destroyed, only he will remain, He is eternal and we bow down before only one God, Allah.

Oh! The lord of Muhammad sallal lahu alaihe wa aalihi wa sallam and Ali Alaihesalam, we declare your Tauheed (Oneness).

Make us also among those witnesses who have testified Tauheed, Risalat and Wilayat and have always tried to follow the footprints of Panjtan Pak.

In this book of mine, I have tried to point out and thereby remove the evils, malpractices spreading in the community, to understand and explain the situation, to fight against the void and to make efforts necessary for a better tomorrow, and at the same time I have requested the children of Rasool Sallallallahu Alaihi wa Sallam i.e Saadat/Sharif/Agha brothers and sisters and the lovers of Ahlebayt Alaihis Salaam and servants of Maula Ali present in this era to understand their responsibilities and guide those sections of the Ummah who are striving to follow the right path.

I always try to write my books in easy, understandable and colloquially language so that even a less educated person can understand it easily. Once again I am trying to give words to my concern and responsibility with the hope that this book of mine will try to wake up the people who are sleeping in ignorance. Allahu Akbar. Allahumma Salle ala Muhammad wa ala aale Muhammad.

ﭖﭖﭖ

Prologue

Assalam o Alaikum wa Rahmatullahe wa Barakatahu.

My dear brothers, sisters, elders and friends! Although I have written this book for the entire Ummah, but the Believing brothers and sisters of the Ummah have more responsibility than others. Similarly, among the brothers and sisters who are the Kalma reciters, I feel the responsibility of Saadat, Syed i.e. Aal e Rasool, Aal-e-Panjatan Pak Alaihis Salam is more than them.

At the time of writing this book, my heart and mind is surrounded amidst many worries. I am worried about the mess that has spread in the society. Everywhere we find people who are just oblivious to religion. It feels as if humanity, honesty, loyalty and goodness is taking its last breath.

It's my heartfelt urge that people of all religions and sects should read this book, but it is specially written for Saadat Hazraat. As a Syed, I feel a kind of right of mine on my Saadat brothers and sisters and I also believe that change begins with oneself and one's own family, and I also believe that a Syed / Saadat being a descent from the lineage of Rasool Allah Sallallahu alaihe wa aalihi wa sallam, is a guide for the entire Ummah.

If a Saadat does not persevere to spread the truth, to oppose the perversion of the community, if he does not take a stand against defending the truth and does not rebel against the void, then how can we criticize the leniency of the Ummah?, If only the people who are called the progeny of Hasnain Kariman Alaihimussalam remain silent then who will raise the flag of Deen-e-Haq?

Who will save Islam at the cost of their own blood?, Who will save the Shariat from shattering?, Who will transform a repenting sinner (who has gone astray) like Hurr from the Yazeedi army to Hurr Alaihis Salam?, Who will spare the life of humanity?, Who will persevere to spread faith and loyalty among the masses?

O The Believers! The people waiting for the appearance of Imam-e-Zamana, Imam-e-Qaayam, Imam Mehdi Alaihissalam (The Awaited One)!

The appearance of the Imam will not take place until you make yourself ready to help the Imam. Illa Masha'Allah.

This book of mine is in true sense,a message for all the Saadats, lovers of Ahlebait (AS) and the entire Ummah. You can also percieve it as a letter written by me for my Saadat brothers and sisters. May Allah Rab ul Izzat guide us to the straight path.

Allahumma Salle Ala Muhammad wa Ala Aale Muhammad.

ڡڡڡ

ONE
KNOW YOURSELF

My loved ones! The Maulvi tells us that a person can attain salvation by realizing the mystic presence of Allah, but he does not tells that the first step for attaining that knowledge is to recognize oneself, that is, if you want to know Allah, you first need to know your inner self. Every being will return to its original self, it means that everything will return to its original form, so it is important that we first start finding ourselves.

"Khudi ko chhor Bande, Khuda talaashte hain,
Aasan ko chhorte hain, mushkil talaashte hain".

Here I do not at all mean that recognition of God is not necessary but I am myself testifying that the main aim of every man's life is to attain conversant of his Lord. But there is always a way of attaining this. One should always try to proceed from easy to the difficult path.

The most basic condition for attaining Marifat-e-Ilahi is that first a person should understand his inner self and then fourteen Innocents (Maasoomeen) because only through these fourteen

Chosen Ones, knowledge of true deen (Marefat,Risalat, Nabuwat, Vilayat, Imamat) has reached the Ummah and these fourteen are the true guiding light for spreading the light of Allah in this world.

I urge my Ahle Saadat brothers and sisters to try to recognize your true self in this short span of life. You are from our Prophet's clan, the progeny of the gate of knowledge, Maula Ali Alaihissalam and Fatima bint e Muhammad Salamullah Alaiha and the descendants of Hasnain Karimain Alaihimussalam. You were supposed to be at the foremost level of religious and worldly knowledge, you were supposed to guide the entire Ummah and you were supposed to readily sacrifice your life and property in defense of the Ahle Bayt Alaihissalam and to fight against the void. But the sad thing is that today some non-saadats bearing the name of saadat and real saadats are also following deceitful clerics and defaming the religion.

In the present era, I find every sect working hard to prove the truthfulness of their clerics, every sect is taking pride in its belief and is determined to convince people in favor of their favorite character in history or should I say, to impose those characters as rightful in the minds of the people.

On the other hand, it is an unfortunate disgrace to see some Saadats considering and calling their own forefather Maula Ali Alaihissalam, the best of mankind after Muhammad Sallallahu Alaihe Wa Aalihi Wa Sallam, the true slave of Lord of Kaaba as the fourth caliph. They even do not refrain themselves from calling their most honorable forefather Sarkar Abu Talib a non believer or Kafir. They are hell-bent on proving their own patron, their own foremother Syeda Fatima Salamullah Alaiha as guilty on the issue of Fadak. More shamefully, they are even calling the murderers of their own father Hasan o Hussain Alaihimussalam as Raziallahanhu that means considering them as those with whom Allah is pleased.

The need of the hour was that we should have taken pride in the Panjtan and Ahlebait Alaihimussalam, spreading their teachings and living and dying for their cause. Although it is not the fault of any one person, in fact this world is such that anyone gets cheated and mesmerized by its glare and starts running after this colorful world.

In the same way, after the demise of Rasool Allah Sallallahu Alaihe Wa Aalihi Wa Sallam, the majority of the Ummah had started efforts to distance people from Ahlebait Alaihimussalam.
Unfortunately even today, the number of Marwani clerics and Yazidi Mullahs is more in comparison to the righteous Ulema-e-Deen-e-Haq.

I consider it useless to talk about non-saadat people who falsely use saadat in their name, because what can be said about the one who has changed his own lineage by not calling himself the son of his own father?
Although I must say that whosoever's child you may be, you should make your identity common by connecting with your parents. Changing one's lineage is a big crime. Moreover, there is no place for casteism in Islam, and different lineages are for mere recognition of each other's identity. Nevertheless when these clerics mislead the people, the majority of the Ummah falls in their trap and goes astray while spoiling their beliefs by following them.

Those Saadats whose parents had lost themselves in the glory of this world and remained heedless about the education and training of their children, when they listen to the speeches of these clerics, the Friday sermons on the pulpit in which they repeatedly deliver made up stories not unfolding the true deen, consider it as the true path of Islam which however is not at all related to Quran, Hadees, Ahlebayt Alaihissalam and the Islamic history.

Although it is a matter of deep regret but we cannot even deny the fact that we Ahle Saadats too, have not been up to the mark in fulfilling our responsibilities in the way it should have been fulfilled. We have also made some mistakes and blunders which should not have happened by us, for example, opting to remain silent on the historical issues of Yazid's father Muawiya, sealing our lips on the issues of Fadak, etc.

The majority of Ummah had forgotten the purpose of the event of Karbala, but we Ahl al-Saadat too restricted the purpose of Karbala to mere mourning, crying and raising slogans. We in fact, to a great extent, have failed to spread the message of Karbala through our deeds.

The present day Maulvis are defending Yazid, Yazid's father and grandfather, defending people like Marwan and Mughira and Ahle Saadat prefer to remain silent. The height of their silence is such that even when the ancestors of Ahle Saadats are criticized and accused, they do not bother to break their silence.

Some Saadats, who became Peers, fear that by speaking the truth, their disciples would decrease, while some Sadats are afraid that people will call them Shia instead of Sunnis.
Some saadats had even crossed their line by blindly following such

peers who themselves are followers of Muaviya.

My Sadat brothers, sisters and all the lovers of Ahlebait Alaihimusallam, I request you all to seek knowledge about your own self, know yourself, dare to distinguish between truth and false and do not be afraid to speak it out and spread it. Emphasize on the right education and upbringing of your children; connect them with the Qur'an and Ahlebait Alaihimussalam because that is the only way that leads to the truth and to God. Teach your progeny the message of Karbala so that they can become followers and true disciples of Imam-e-Zamana, Imam-e-Qayam.

Allahu Akbar Kaseeran Kaseera. Allahumma salle ala Muhammad wa ala Aale Muhammad.

"Falsafi ko behes ke andar khuda milta nahi,
Dor ko suljha raha hai aur sira milta nahi
Marefat khaliq ki aalam mein bohot dushwaar hai,
Sheher e tan mein jab ki khud apna pata milta nahi".

ᐅᐅᐅ

TWO
DEFEND BLATANTLY

First of all, the need of the hour is to bring out the true picture of Islam in front of the people because some ignorant people who call themselves Muslims and clerics who consider themselves as promoters of Deen e Haqq have presented a wrong image of Islam to the world because of which people of other religions look down upon it with hatred .Here too I believe that the fault is ours, mine, all Ahle Saadat and that of the lovers of Ali Alaihissalam (Shian e Ali)because blaming others is the way of cowards and Yazidi clerics have worked really hard to serve their nefarious purpose in every era and until now. People who have nothing to do with Islam are being presented as heroes/warriors and par humans of Islam, and we Saadat and lovers of Ahlebayt Alaihissalam are not able to spread the truth in a way it should have been done.

Allah Rabb ul Izzat has mentioned in the Holy Qur'an -

Indeed Islam is the only true deen closer to Allah. (Part of verse 19 of Surah Al-Imran)

If we contemplate on this verse, we will realize that there are many types of Islam, one is true Islam and the others are false Islam. The true Islam is that which Allah Rabb ul Izzat gave to us through His Prophet and which was followed by fourteen Maasoomeen and Twelve Imams, and the second one which is present in our homes. True Islam is just one true religion, but there are many types of false/fake Islams. People have started many innovations in the name of Islam and have also hidden many truths and facts. The hypocrite, careless men and ignorant women, are the ones who gradually kept making such drastic changes in the religion resulting to a completely morphed religion that is now found in our homes different from the true one.

I have already written a book on this topic, in which I have explained in detail about Takhliqi Deen and Haqiqi Deen. In the book I have tried my best to explain that why and how a false Islam has been raised against the true one. What are its disadvantages and how it has affected the society, and how will people be saved from Takhliqi Deen and brought to Haqiqi Deen, etc?

To know all these issues in detail, you really need to read my book 'Do Islam'.
However, here I am speaking about defending openly. All my Ahle Saadat and followers of Ali Alaihissalam brothers and sisters, when the enemies of Ahlebait Alaihimusallam are openly defending Yazid, his father and grandfather, and are trying to prove them exalted who fled leaving the Prophet(Sallalahu Alaihi Wa Alaihi Wassalam), alone in the battlefield, then why are we lagging behind in defending Panjatan O Ahlebait Alaihimusallam?

When ignorant, illiterate self made Mullahs bark against Hazrat Abu Talib, why is the truth not defended by us? When the daughter of our Prophet Sallalahu Alaihi Wa Alaihi Wassalam is accused everyday on the issue of Baag e Fadak and Hasnain Karimain is targeted and our Imams especially Imam e Qayyam Alaihissalam is also spoken against but we choose to remain silent? This is shameful and soul frightening for us.

I believe that we should speak things that divides the ummah, nor should sectarianism be widespread, but this does not mean that we cease to speak the truth or ignore the false just to maintain the unity of the ummah. My loved ones! The period of silence is over, now we have to respond to every voice, objections, false and baseless accusations raised against Ahlebait Alaihimusallam.

I have been saying this for a long time, whether they are Yazidi clerics who spoil people's faith under the guise of Islam, or they are hypocrites who intend to mislead the slaves of Ali Alaihissalam by calling themselves Maulai, there are two big nooses around their necks. They save themselves from every situation but get trapped on these two issues, one is the issue of Fadak and the other is the faith and belief of Hazrat Abu Talib.Trying to prove Maula Ali Alaihissalam as fourth Caliph and proving the status of Ahlebait Alaihimusallam to be less than Sahaba or equal to Sahaba is also a great sign of these hypocrite.

My Saadat and Ghulam-e Ahlebait brothers and sisters! Today is the era when Yazidi followers of Muaviya are not ashamed to call themselves Yazidis, so why should we hesitate to raise the flag of truth and righteousness??

Spread the truth from the pulpits, if you do not find any platform or pulpit; try to spread the truth first among your near ones, friends and family. It is not always a condition to hold a large-scale gathering every time to spread the message of Islam. Wherever a group of ten to twenty people sit and discuss and spread truth that is a Majlis, that is a Mehfil (Gathering).

• 9 •

Moreover if that too seems difficult then at least work on yourself, on your wives and children and dedicate yourself and your offspring to the Nusrat of Imam e Zamana, Imam e Qayam.

"Haq parasti ko yahan kaun hai Aamada e daar,
Kis ko taufiq hai be gaur o kafan hone ki."

ݒݒݒ

THREE

Aqeedah of Imam Hasan Alaihissalam

Many people who write Syed in their names and many such people who really belong to the Saadat family, but they are the only ones who do not consider Hazrat Ali Alaihissalam to be the foremost after Prophets, rather claim some other personality to be the first and foremost after the prophets and many of our Maulai brothers and sisters also hold similar belief.

I will not mention the name, but there is a very famous Syed Sahab in India who once attacked the faith of Hazrat Abu Talib (although he later confessed and corrected his act), sometimes he gave statements in defense of Muawiya, and in other times tried to prove some other Sahaba superior than Maula Ali Alaihissalam. The most surprising fact is that he claims that he is a Hasani Saadat, that means, his father is from the progeny of Imam Hasan Alaihissalam.I am not discriminating between Hasani and Hussaini Saadat that both of you have different beliefs, in fact, Imam Hasan Alaihissalam is the Imam of Imam Hussain alaihissalam too and is called Hujjatullah after Maula Ali Alaihissalam.

If we look at the six authentic books of hadees (Sihah Sittah) of Ahle Sunnah wal Jamaat, then we find a hadith in it, the narrator of which is Imam Hasan himself. The hadith is something like this -

(Narrators of the Hadith, Ishaaq bin Ibrahim, An-Nazr bin Shumail, Younus bin Abu Ishaaq, Hubairah bin Yarim.)

When Hazrat Ali Alaihissalam, father of Syed Imam Hasan Alaihissalam, was assassinated, Imam Hasan was wearing a black Imamah (turban). He assembled the people and said, "In the few days gone by you people have martyred that person, whose place neither people who came before him could take nor those who come after him can ever match his level. And our Rasulullah Sallallahu Alayhi Wasallam said for him, Tomorrow I will hand over the flag to a person who loves Allah and His Messenger, and Allah and His Messenger love him and Gabriel (Jibril) fights for him on his right and Michael on his left. And then the flag will not return until Allah Tabaraq wa Ta'ala gives him victory. He did not leave any dinars or dirhams, except seven hundred dirhams which he took from his earnings, with which he intended to buy a servant for his household."

In the given hadith, that sermon is mentioned which was delivered by the elder son of Maula Ali Alaihissalam i.e. Imam Hasan Alaihissalam after his martyrdom, which clearly indicates that even Imam Hasan Alaihissalam believed that after Rasool Allah Sallalahu Alaihi Wassalam,Maula Ali Alaihissalam was the foremost in honor and status and there is not an inch of doubt that after Maula Ali Alaihissalam, Imam Hasan has the highest status and he is 'Hujjatullah'.

He is the patron of all Hasani, Husayni, Hasani-Husayni, Husayni-Hasani Saadat and whether it is Imam Hussain Alaihissalam or the progeny of Hasnain Karimain, no one's faith can be distinct from the faith and belief of Imam Hasan Alaihissalam.

Now here the matter of concern is that when Maula Ali is the foremost as per the belief of Imam Hasan Alaihissalam, then why have some Saadats who call themselves the children of Imam Hasan Alaihissalam, deviated from the path of their own father and formed their own belief? , How can some people who call themselves lovers of Ahlebait Alaihimusallam, separate from Imam Hasan Alaihissalam and create their own faith?

Jinko aata nahi duniya mein koi fan tum ho
Nahi jis qaum ko parwa e nasheman tum ho
Bijliyan jisme ho aasuda wo khirman tum ho
Bech khate hain jo aslaaf ke madfan tum ho.

A Saadat always remains a Saadat, whether the world calls him Sunni or Shia, it doesn't matter. A Saadat's job is to spread the truth, a real Saadat, stays miles away from sectarianism and keeps on spreading the truth and lives and dies for Islam. I want to tell to the Saadats that if sectarian clerics oppose Ahlulbayt Alaihimusallam, then we should also come forward in the defense of Ahlulbayt Alaihissalam. In actual, this should be the responsibility of the entire Ummah, but most of the Ummah is busy following the Yazidi clerics, but the responsibility of the Saadats is greater in every respect because they are not only the Ummah but also the progeny. Every finger pointed at Ahlebait Alaihimusallam is like an attack on our ancestors, every small and large, false accusation of Yazidi clerics should be abandoned and I believe every Saadat should act as a counsel and defender of Ahlebayt Alaihimusallam.

The eminent Ulema, Musannif, Muarrikh and Muhaddith of Ahle Sunnat Wal Jamaat have clearly written in their books that there was a Jamaat among the Companions of the Prophet Sallallahu Alayhi Wa Alaihi Wa Sallam who believed in the superiority of Maula Ali Alaihis Salam. Hazrat Salman Farsi, Hazrat Abuzar Ghaffari, Hazrat Miqdad, Hazrat Malik al-Ashtar, Hazrat Ammar, Hazrat Bilal, Hazrat Hujr, Hazrat Muhammad bin Abu Bakr etc. also considered Hazrat Ali Alaihissalam as the foremost after Rasool Allah Sallalahu Alaihi Wassalam.

My dear ones! There have been two types of beliefs in Ahle Sunnat wal Jamaat, the one who considers Maula Ali Alaihissalam as superior and the other one who considers the first caliph of the Ummah as superior. The elders of Ahle Sunnat wal Jamaat and their ulemas accepted both the beliefs as correct, but then a group emerged in the Sunni section that started calling its Maulvis superior and considered themselves as governors of Islam, declaring themselves believers and rebuking others as Kafirs (Non believers).This awful sect presented itself as a lover of the Prophet, but gradually turned the Ummah against his progeny, their real aim was to impose their own Maulvis on everyone. The defenders of Ali Alaihissalam and Ahlulbayt came to be called Shia-Rafzi-Kafir. Behind the veil of the name and honor of the Sahabas(Companions of Rasulullah Sallallahu Alayhi Wasallam)only four to six Sahabas were held high and their names were propagated and millions of other faithful Sahabas were ignored, the maulayis who disobeyed these four-six Sahabas were called Gustakh-e Sahaba and thus gradually the condition of the Ummah turned from bad to worse.

My Comrades! Our Prophet Muhammad Sallallahu Alayhi Wa Alihi Wa Sallam did not leave us without a guardian rather before leaving this world for the heavenly abode,he declared that, "Whomsoever considers me as his Maula ,Ali is also his Maula." And he, the Messenger of God, have commanded us to hold on to two important things, the Qur'an and the Ahl al-Bayt.

Of course, adherence to the Qur'an and Ahlebait is the only straight path and the only way to Truth. It is not necessary to hold on to anything else except these two.

Allahumma Salle Ala Muhammad Wa Ala Aale Muhammad.

Baap ka ilm na bete ko agar azbar ho,
    Phir pisar kaabil e miraas e pidar kyun kar ho?

ᗊᗊᗊ

FOUR
SELF-IMPROVEMENT

Do you know what the most difficult thing in the world is? To criticize yourself, to admit your mistakes, to repent and to turn to the truth. This task becomes even more difficult when it comes to your belief. To criticize the belief that you and your family are following, to criticize that belief for which you have argued with others not once but hundreds of times, is really a very difficult task and only a courageous and conscientious person can do it.

My dear ones! We did not come to this world for remaining egotist, but the real and basic purpose of our life is only to follow and spread righteousness. If we are on the wrong track of faith we need to accept the truth, repent openly and try to reform our beliefs and spread the truth by following the right path for the rest of our life. Today, superficial (Takliqi) deen is spread all around and the majority of the Ummah is ignorant of the actual (Haqiqi) Deen. The bitter fact is that people now consider Takhliqi deen as the actual one and real or Haqiqi deen is like a new and unknown thing being served to them. It is not a great sin to be led astray under the influence of such circumstances and satanism, but not to investigate, not to search for the truth, to stick to false beliefs and lies despite having understood the truth, is a great sin. Our effort should not be to be right in the eyes of the world, but our effort should be to please our Lord (Allah).

Whether you belong to Ahle Sunnat wal Jamaat or Ahle Tashayyo, it is necessary to follow the right path and spread truth in every situation. I never encourage that one should abuse or talk dirty about any historical personality like an incompetent and ridiculous person but while staying in the ambit of Shari'a, spread what is right, even if it is against our belief.For example, I never say that one should speak ill of the first or the second Caliph, but whenever the issue of Fadak arises, it should always be said openly that not giving the land of Fadak to the daughter of Rasulullah Sallallahu Alayhi Wasallam was a big mistake not only of the Caliph but all the Muslims present in that era and similarly the third caliph also made a big mistake by giving that same land of fadak to his own daughter.

My loved ones! Respect of any person has its place, but it does not mean that we should stop accusing the wrong in the name of respect. The biggest beauty of our Islam is that we Muslims are righteous and if we have to go against our own father or son for the sake of righteousness, we do not step back. It should be the work of a Muslim to raise his voice for justice, to support the oppressed and to be the sigh of the afflicted. And then there is not an inch of doubt that in this Ummah of Muhammad Sallallahu Alaihi Wa Alaihi Wa Sallam, if there is anyone who is the most oppressed, persecuted, sorrowful, then they are the Ahlebait of Rasool Sallallahu Alaihi Wa Alaihi Wa Sallam.

Those who disobey the order of Rasoolullah Sallallahu Alaihi Wa Alaihi Wa Sallam and take decisions according to their own mind are also guilty, those who did not give her rights to Rasoolullah's daughter Fatima Salamullah Alaiha and those who remain silent seeing her rights being denied are also guilty. Those who fought against Maula ALI Alaihissalam are futile, those who usurped the rights of Hazrat Imam Hasan Alaihissalam, those who broke the peace treaty, those who surrounded and killed Hazrat Imam Hussain Alaihissalam and martyred and chopped the offsprings of Rasool into pieces and every hidden and visible enemy of the Ahlebait who was involved in the murder are the biggest culprits of this Ummah. And there is no forgiveness for those who associate others with Allah or those who disbelieve.

Instead of blindly following any sect, we should try to read and understand each and every sect. There are two major groups in Islam, Ahle Sunnat wal Jamaat and Ahle Tashayyo, the rest of the sects that have emerged are their divisions. There is less conflict and more conspiracy between these two gangs or groups. To know about this in detail, you can read a book written by me named "Shia-Sunni".

However, the cleric of every religious school wants that the people of his sect should read and listen to the scholars of the same school, not because he is worried about your Hereafter, but there are two important reasons behind this. The first reason is money laundering, yes my dear ones! You may find it strange to hear, but this is a bitter reality, most of the religious clerics practice sectarianism only to run the business of donations, if you leave their sect and join another one, they are afraid that their income will get hampered.The second reason is the ignorance of the cleric. If you start reading about ten more sects then questions will start arising in your heart and mind, you will start seeing the shortcomings of your sect and also the merits of other ones, which cannot be tolerated by Yazidi Mullahs. It will not be possible nor will they be able to answer you, that's why they have already closed that way ,they stop people from education, stop them from studying and investigating, then questions will be nipped in the bud itself.

So my brothers and sisters! Keep reading as much as you can, read books of every sect, keep gaining knowledge in the light of Quran, History, Hadith and Teachings of Ahlebait Alaihimussalam, keep investigating, start questioning, start taking steps towards the truth and when you start realizing your mistake, then accept the truth with a true repentance and start spreading the truth.

"Tauba ka yahi waqt hai kya soch rahe ho,
Sajde mein jabeenon ko jhuka kyun nahin dete,
Ye jhoote khuda mil ke dubo denge safeena ,
Tum haadee-e-bar-haq ko sada kyun nahin dete."

ᐯᐯᐯ

FIVE

IMPORTANCE OF EDUCATION

A lot of donations are taken in the name of mosques and madrasas, but all the money is spent in decorating the mosques and filling their coffers. It is a matter of great regret that except a few school, college and university, the Muslims of India could not build their own schools, colleges and universities.If not many,at least a school can be made in every district, a college in every division and a university in every state, in which good training / education / education can be given free of cost or at least by charging a nominal fee. Along with religious education, worldly education can also be provided. Some clerics in our community have planted a point of view in people's mind of giving religious education to children, which is useful in both worlds, worldly education is not necessary, but in fact every better knowledge is from Allah. Here it is necessary to understand one thing first, that while living in the world, living your life according to the commands of Allah and Rasoolullah, living by holding the teachings of Quran and Ahlebait Alaihimussalam is religion.Religion and world seem different from each other, but they are connected with each other and both aren't different at all.

One more regretful thing, which arose in my mind while contemplating is that some people of our community send their children to madrasas in the name of religious education, but they lag behind in imparting worldly education and Mullah ji , in the name of religion, only teaches student to read Quran in Arabic, neither its Tafsir or Tarjuma(meaning) nor Hadiths, nor the principles of Shariat or history of Islam are taught. As a result, the child neither has the knowledge of religion nor of the world and he becomes unsuccessful in both the worlds.

My loved ones! Every parent should give the basic knowledge of religion to their children. Parents and teachers should pay heed to the correct education and training of the child and make the child a pious and better human being. A child should be taught Quran, Hadiths, teachings of Ahlebait Alaihimussalam and at least he should be taught that much knowledge that he learns to differentiate between Halal and Haram, but it is not necessary that you make every child a scholar of religion.The child must have basic religious knowledge which is used in daily life, should also be able to perform the prayers, but when other big issues arise, he can ask the Ulema.

Of course! Our community needs good Ulema but our community also needs good doctors, engineers, teachers, professors, traders, entrepreneurs, lawyers, mechanics, computer operators, researchers, scientists, etc. How much better it would be if there are teachers, professors etc. in our society who perform salat, who along with religious education and worship,also imparts worldly education to children and make them a better human being. There should be doctors, engineers etc. who pay zakat, who help the poor and orphans. How much better it would be if someone becomes a scientist as well as a Haji. But the Yazidi clerics, for their own benefit, have separated the education of religion and the world and have erected a wall of ignorance and mental slavery between the two.

"Mudda tera agar duniya mein hai taleem-e-deen ,
 Tark-e-duniya qaum ko apni na sikhlana kahin"

My loved ones! Allah is the creator and all others are the creation of Allah. If you would have contemplated about the creations of Allah, you would surely have been surprised. For example, Allah created the Sun and gave it to his servants, Sun is a big source of energy, which generates natural energy, this is also a great blessing of Allah Rab ul Izzat.The sad thing is that it is we Muslims who have not learned to use this great blessing.Today many things like solar geyser, solar cooker, solar battery, solar car, solar inverter etc. have been invented, but our community is still lagging behind in such inventions. If we ponder, we will find that today we are lagging behind in every field, we are unsuccessful, even more surprising is that we belong to that community, in which people like Jabir Ibn e Hayyan disciple of Imam Jafar Sadiq Alaihissalam was born, who is known to the world as Father of ancient chemistry. Then what can we say about the knowledge and wisdom of Ahlebait Alaihimussalam and progeny of Rasool Sallallahu Alaihi wa Aalihi Wasallam, when their disciples turn out to be so much superior in knowledge.Knowledge is also for Allah and it is necessary that we acquire education and training for the sake of Allah and use it to benefit the world and all creatures.

"Taleem ka shor aisa, tehzeeb ka gul itna
Barkat jo nahi hoti, niyat ki kharabi hai"

Muslims claim that we have the last book sent by Allah and in that book there are messages and verses of God and entire knowledge of this world is present in this book but it is a pity to find that the Ummah has forgotten that this Book of Allah begins with "Iqra". And iqra means to read (read/recite), but we have distanced ourselves from both religious and worldly education.Let me state one more thing here that along with academic education,attention should also be paid to skills, be it boys or girls of the community, along with studies, skills must also be learned, such as sewing, embroidery, carpentry,art, etc. Remember one more thing, when Imam Mehdi Alaihissalam will reappear, along with religious scholars, the support of Muslim scientists, researchers, doctors, engineers, teachers, professors, tradesmen, entrepreneurs, lawyers, mechanic, computer operator, ethical hacker, etc. will also be required. The victory of Imam Mehdi Alaihissalam does not only mean to excel in religious knowledge and lag in worldly one.

My loved ones! Keep gaining knowledge because there is no age to gain knowledge and at the same time keep trying and working hard for the right education and training of your children. Give good education and training to your sons so that the condition of your house improves and impart good training and education to your daughters so that the progeny of a family improves.

"Zindagi ho meri parvaan ki surat Ya Rab,
Ilm ki shamma se ho mujh ko mohabbat Ya Rab".

ᐳᐳᐳ

SIX

MOSQUES AND LIBRARIES

Mosques and mosque committees will also have to play an important role in the education of our children. Instead of spending much on the decoration of the mosque, more attention should be paid to building a library in the mosque. Every mosque must have a seminary and a library and there must be a scholar who can be present in the library at least for a few hours, if not more, and answer people's questions.

The library should contain all kinds of books related to religion, world, children's overall education, subjects related to school etc. In fact, I urge that even the poorest of the poor Muslim should keep aside 50-100 rupees a month and save 600-1200 rupees in a year to buy books for himself or give them to his children. If someone has ample money, then he can gradually strive to build a small library in his house too. One should not talk unnecessarily in the mosque and definitely shouldn't speak during Salat/Namaz, but some clerics scare the youth and children to such an extent that the youth and children start mistaking it as a sin to utter a single word in the mosque, whereas the youth should be taught that they can sit inside their respective mosques and initiate discussions with each other regarding improvement of the community, betterment of society.They can discuss about religious and worldly knowlegde, discuss political affairs, and also about the development of the community-city-country.

Those mosques which do not have library and seminaries (Madrasas)and due to poor financial condition of the committee, it may take time to build them, then at least arrangements should be made for children to study in the mosques, especially at the time of examinations. The children should be allowed to study in the mosques from about 7 o'clock after Fajr till 12 o'clock before Zuhr.You can also do the same between Zuhr to Asr from 2:15-4:15 and if the children reside near the mosque, then after Isha, open the mosques to the children till 9:15-11. This means that ultimately, for about 6-7 hours we can give the children of our community a clean place, quiet environment, and necessities like air, lighting etc.

You might feel that all this necessities can be given at home as well. So my loved ones! Everyone's financial status is not the same, there are some of our brothers who find it difficult to even make both ends meet for themselves and their families, their houses are not big enough, and there is no proper arrangement for electricity, lighting and air. If we provide facilities to them through mosques, then their children will also get an opportunity to become successful after being educated and will grow up to serve the community and country.Along with the arrangements for the education of the children, if an educated youth is appointed in the mosque for their guidance then the children will also be protected and supervised and at the same time, if they are unable to understand anything, he can resolve their queries.

Since my childhood, I have heard orations (Takreer) before the Friday sermon in the mosques of Ahle Sunnat wal Jamaat.The subject of these orations is mostly the daily prayers, the virtues of four-six companions of Rasoolullah Sallallahu Alaihi Wa Alaihi Wassalam, the five pillars of Islam etc. I am not saying at all that these are not right, but sometimes subjects such as the upbringing and education of children, on moral values, on transformation of a man into true human, on the rights of parents, wives and children, on the rights of brothers and sisters, relatives and neighbours should also be discussed from the pulpit.

There should also be a discussion on the evils and ignorance spread in marriages, eradicating dowry system and extravagance rituals, the participation of Muslims in politics, the widespread corruption in society and efforts to deal with them.

A mosque is the house of God, which is undoubtedly a place of worship, but this is the same sacred place where a child comes and becomes a man and gradually transforms into a human being, a Muslim, a believer. It is not that important what we are leaving behind for our children, but what matters is what we are leaving in our children. If your child grows up to be a good person, a good Muslim, a good believer, has knowledge of the religion and the world, is morally and ethically equipped, talented, virtuous, observant, learned and wise, then surely you have succeeded. May Allah Rabb ul Izzat grant us the ability to perform more than listening and speaking. Grant us Success in the world and the hereafter. My dear ones! Remember, the only way to success is to hold on to the Qur'an and Ahlebait Alaihimusallam.

Allahumma Salle Ala Muhammad wa Ala Aale Muhammad.

"Ilm hai insaan ki tehzeeb-o-tamaddun ke liye,
Ye nahi insaani qadron ke talavvun ke liye.
Ilm hai aapas mein ikhlaas-o-ukhuvvat ke liye,
Ye nahi auron ke nuqsaan-o-halaakat ke liye.
Ilm hai insaan ke bahbood-o-baqa ke waaste,
Ye nahi insaaniyat ki ibtila ke waaste.
Ilm hai insaan ki khud-aagahi ke waaste,
aur insaanon mein bhai chaargi ke waaste .
Ilm se raushan khayaali aati hai insaan mein,
Pukhtagi akhlaaq mein to taazgi imaan mein .
Ilm badhta hai koi usko ghata sakta nahi,
Ye wo daulat hai jise koi chura sakta nahi.
Ilm ko failaiye acche maqaasid ke liye,
Taaki duniya ki taraqqi ka nishaana badh sake.
Ilm chadhta aaftaab aur ilm hai baad-e-muraad,
Ilm zindaabaad is ki aaghi painda-baad".

ᖁᖁᖁ

SEVEN

ART, SPORTS AND PHYSICAL EXERCISE

My dear ones! Along with education of children, sports and physical exercise are also very important. Make sure to engage your children in at least one indoor and one outdoor game/play. Kabaddi, badminton, wrestling, boxing etc. are called indoor games, while football, cricket, hockey etc. are called outdoor games. Sports also lead to the physical development of children; the child learns sportsmanship and becomes stronger mentally-physically. It is better for a child to sleep early at night and wake up early in the morning. Even after waking up, it is important to walk, run, exercise, and keep yourself active. Cycling, swimming etc. are also good for the child, although while learning swimming etc. it is important that the child is supervised by the parents and a good swimmer. Children should make it a habit to play sports and exercise regularly in the morning and evening.Apart from this, children should go for a walk for at least 15-20 minutes after eating,i.e. a small walk at a normal speed. It is really beneficial for health and digestion.

If you feel that your child is not good in academics but is interested in any sport, then let him pursue that sport as well. It is also true that such children are rarely seen who tend to study by themselves, especially in the beginning, in early stages of childhood. So try to get the child to study but at the same time let him play the sports in which he is interested.

Now I want to discuss a little about art as well.I have seen many children who were average in studies but excelled in art. Someone is good at painting; someone excels in art and craft, while someone writes well, or is good at embroidery, sewing and so on. So my loved ones! Let your children learn skills and arts as well, along with studies because many times children can make their identity on the basis of their arts and skills. Considering the current scenario, it is also important that if it is possible for you, teach your children to drive two-wheeled vehicles such as scooters, scooty, motorcycles and four-wheeled vehicles such as cars, jeeps, etc. when they become adults. I have often seen that people look down on mechanics whereas there is nothing wrong with children learning repairing and mechanical work as a skill, be it mobiles, TVs, computer or a laptop, they often need repairing. Electric fittings, water fittings, motors, machineries too need installation and repair for which mechanics, electricians etc. are required and will continue to do so.

We should teach our children fencing; horse-riding, boxing, wrestling, shooting and even cudgelling.My loved ones! Keep trying to give and get your children trainings of art, sports and skills as much as possible. May Allah Rab ul Izzat grant us all the ability to act more than listen or tell.
Allahu Akbar Kaseeran Kaseera.

Allahumma Salle Ala Muhammad wa Ala Aale Muhammad.

"Gulami mein na kaam aati hai shamsheerein na tadbeerein,
   Jo ho zauq-e-yaqeen paida to kat jaati hain zanjeerein.
Koi andaaza kar sakta hai us ke zor-e-baazu ka,
   Nigaah-e-mard-e-momin se badal jaati hain taqdeerein.
   Sabaq phir padh sadaaqat ka, adaalat ka,shujaat ka,
Liya jaega tujh se kaam duniya ki Imaamat ka".

❧❧❧

EIGHT

IMPROVEMENT IN DIET

I will write this topic in two parts, first I will discuss about halal-haraam (permissible and non permissible) foods and then I will talk about those Halal items which we should have eaten but because of our carelessness we are bereft of the blessings of Allah. My dear ones! The most important thing to be kept in mind while eating and drinking is that the food should be halal, haram should be avoided at all costs. The things that Allah and his Messenger have declared as halal are permissible and the things that have been declared as haram are not. For example, goat meat is halal and pig meat is haram. There is a list of food items halal and haraam foods about which you can read from Quran and Hadith in detail. It is often seen that Muslims are very cautious about halal and haram foods but they forget that the halal food bought with haram earnings is also haram, and in this way they along with their children are being fed haram.

Whenever someone asks me what is the condition to get the right education or training? I answer that first of all it is important to correct your intakes i.e. eat halal things earned from halal money. Otherwise, there will be complications in getting education or training and even if you get the knowledge you will not be able to implement it in the right way. So my brothers and sisters! Feed your body with pure, clean, halal foods and also feed the same to your children so that they can flourish outwardly and inwardly as well.

Now let's talk about what should be eaten? So,Normally all of us eat grains like wheat, rice, pulses, etc., as well as meat,fish,eggs etc.and all of these things are halal too, but foods such as dry fruits are either left out or are taken in a very less quantity even though these things are more beneficial to eat. We should, as per our financial condition,try to include some quantity of dry fruits like dates, almonds, cashews, raisins, chironji, figs, pistachios etc.in our diet.We should also eat fruits like pomegranate, apple, orange, banana etc. Eat seasonal fruits like mango, watermelon, melon, seasonal fruits etc. Also include coconut and peanuts etc. in the diet. Apart from this, eat sprouted beans or sprouted pulses, chickpeas etc. Eat a fiber-rich diet and take care of the rest of the nutritional value of your foods as well. Green vegetables, paneer, curd, buttermilk are also beneficial and dosa, uttapam, semolina cheela, idli etc. or those in which yeast is raised, such food items are also good for our health.

Drink as much water as possible. This does not mean that one has to drink too much water, but that much as to avoid dehydration. For example, an adult should drink 10 to 12 glasses of water and a child of 4 to 8 years should drink 5 to 6 glasses of water and a child of 10-13 years should drink 7-8 glasses of water. Glasses can also be of different sizes but generally there a glass of 8 ounce (fluid ounce) i.e. about 236 ml is used. Here you also need to remember that if you take more liquid diet in your food, then you will drink less water, if you work less, you will also drink less. However, your body itself gives indication to your brain whether you are thirsty or not, whether you need water or not, so save yourself from dehydration.

Eating too much food is also harmful and using too much oil and spices is also not good for health. It is better to maintain a balanced diet and diet does not mean to stop eating something but it means to eat everything in a limit. For example, if you eat some heavy-spicy-oily food one time, you should eat light food in the next half of the day.Avoid consuming fast foods every day but eat them once in a while.It is better to eat an inch less than your hunger. Eating a small quantity of meals taking frequent breaks is more beneficial than gulping down a large meal at a time. Try to eat and drink in a sitting position and always try to drink small amounts of water before and during meals.

If you improve your own habits and make yourself a better person, then you will be able to make your children a better person as well. Correct your and your children's eating habits because a healthy body keeps the mind and heart healthy. This will prove to be beneficial for you as well as your children.
Allahu Akbar Kaseeran Kaseera.

"Ki jinko lat hai haraam khaane ki,
Unhein halaal ki khushboo talak nahin milti."

ᐳᐳᐳ

NINE
UPBRINGING OF CHILDREN

My loved ones! In the current era, parents has to fulfill a dual responsibility, first is to give their children the right education and upbringing, to make them a good human and the other is to protect them from worldly misguidance and from the evils that are spread in the society. In this era where behind the veil of modernism people are moving towards evil doings, to save and prove oneself is a big task in itself. Then it is gradually becomeing even more difficult to guide the children towards the right and prevent them from evil, but it is very important to do so.

Remember My brothers,Allah Rabb ul Izzat has given us only one life and in this one life we have to improve our Naama-e-Amaal(deeds), we also have to work hard to run the expenses of the house, we also have to educate our wives and children and also fulfill our responsibilities for the Ummah. It is the duty of every parent to give at least that much education to make their children capable of understanding the difference between halal and haram (permissible and non permissible).

The upbringing of children, I am trying to highlight this subject from the beginning. One thing is common in our society that children start learning from the age of 7-8 years, some people say 4-5 years, some say 10 years, but the truth is that children starts grasping things from the mother's womb itself. If you read the lives of various saints, you will find that such and such a saint was a born saint, but you will never think about his parents, how were they?Indeed, one whose father is Syed Khwaja Ghiyasuddin and whose mother is Syeda Ummul Wara, then the child becomes Syed Khwaja Moinuddin Chishti.

Anyways, when the child is in the mother's womb, it gets nourishment only from the mother's food, so first of all, it is important to pay attention to one's food, to eat clean and halal food. The cleanliness and piousness of the mother's soul is of utter importance.

When the child is in the womb of the mother, he/she also listens and learns a lot through the mother. Now if a mother reads and recites Quran, Hamd, Naat, Manqabat, Nohas and Marsiyas during her pregnancy the child whom she will give birth to will have a different type of pious nature,inversely if she listens and watch lustful movies and songs, sedition-filled serials, bad web series, then the child born from her will also be worthless.

My loved ones! When Allah, Rabb ul Izzat, blesses His servants with the blessing of children, He also gives many qualities and characteristics in that child, but unfortunately, due to the negligence, carelessness and ignorance of the parents, those qualities and characteristics gradually disappear and vanish. When the child is in the mother's womb, these qualities start to disappear and by the time the child is two-three years old, these qualities fade upto 80% and the remaining qualities are finished by the age of six-seven years. This means that where it should have happened that parents should increase the good characteristics and qualities of their children, its reverse happens; the reason is distance from religion, distance from Qur'an and Ahlebait Alaihimusallam.

People are often heard people saying that children do not have brains, children are goofy, and they do not understand anything, but this is completely inaccurate. Children possess the highest grasping power, even more than the youth. For example,a child learns to speak, eat, walk etc. by watching his parents and the people around him,he does not need to be explained separately that he should use his mouth for eating, he takes food to his mouth by himself, never tries to eat through ears or nose because he constantly learns by seeing his surroundings.

If the child is taught Qur'an, Hadith, teachings of Ahlebait Alaihimusallam,manners, knowledge, good deeds right from the mother's womb until the child reaches adulthood, then surely the children will grow up to be exemplary, In Sha Allah.

Remember one more thing here, as a parent, our duty should be to give our children the right education and upbringing, keep trying to make them a better person and we should not lag behind in our efforts in doing so and keep praying to Allah that our progeny remains steadfast on the path of truth, remain righteous, virtuous, true and good. After doing all this, In Sha Allah, the children will turn out well.

Also remember that a son of Hazrat Adam Alaihissalam killed his own brother, a son of Hazrat Noah Alaihissalam did not support his own father and went astray, some of the sons of Hazrat Yaqub Alaihissalam also wronged their own brother, Hazrat Yusuf Alaihissalam and oppressed him, so even after giving 100% of your efforts, if your children do not turn out to be good, then it is surely not your fault. Let me give you an example, if you are a gardener and your children are its plants, then as a gardener it is important that you take care of every plant, monitor it, give it proper sunlight and water, protect it from harsh weather and animals, fertilize it from time to time, but if the plant does not grow well, it is not your fault at all.

A mother has always been a child's first teacher and a child starts learning from his mother itself.The father often stays out of the house to earn, works hard all day and the child spends most of his time with his mother, so a mother plays a crucial role in the upbringing of a child and she has the biggest role in making the child a better person. That's why I always say that the piousness of the mother is important in making the child virtuous. Often the children of noble mothers turn out to be noble.

If we look through the history, we will find that in the earlier times, the custom of polygamy was common and there have been many people whose sons from one wife were nobler and worthy and those from the other wife turned out to be sinners, because a child learns the most from his mother. The sisters and daughters of the Ummah need to understand their responsibility and strive to fulfill it accordingly.

"Maaon ki gaflat se jab bachchon ko pahunchega gazand,
    Jab fugaan be-tarbiyat aulaad ki hogi buland"

My loved ones! Children learn most of the things on their own by watching their parents, so the parents should work hard on themselves, make themselves pious, virtuous, improve their character, improve their way of speaking, follow the Sunnahs. If you are seen reciting the Qur'an, then your children will automatically develop an inclination towards reading the Qur'an, if you keep yourself busy in the remembrance of Allah Rab ul Izzat, Rasoolullah Sallallahu Alaihe Wa Alaihi Wa Sallam, Panjtan and Ahlebait Alaihimusallam then your children will also be inclined towards this direction.On the contrary if you, remain busy in watching T.V, using mobile, then your children will also insist on doing the same.

"Gharon ki tarbiyat kya aa gyi TV k haathon me,
Koi bachha ab apne baap k upar nahi jata".

The girls of the community, who got married just a few years back and have been blessed with children by Allah, make another big mistake, when the children cry, they let them play with the mobile phone or play videos in it, this absolves them of their responsibility and the child becomes quiet as a result. Gradually, this practice takes the form of addiction and both mother and child get addicted to it. Whether the mother has some work or the child is crying, or if he annoys her, she finds this the easiest way to pacify and amuse her child and the child also gets addicted to watching or playing with the mobile everyday or several times a day.But unfortunately when the child cannnot get off this addiction on growing up, then its the parents who get annoyed the most.

My loved ones! The upbringing of children is a big responsibility in itself and our efforts of today decides how our progeny will be shaped. Give proper education and training to your children so that they can do something better in the way of religion, for the world, the Ummah and themselves, become a pious person and be successful in the world and the hereafter. My brothers, sisters and friends, connect your children with Quran and Ahlebait Alaihimussalam, this is the only way to success.

Allahu Akbar Kaseeran Kaseera.

Allahumma Salle Ala Muhammad wa Ala Aale Muhammad.

"Tarbiyat khoon me rach jaye to tab hota hai,
  Warna aasan nahi jana kisi Karbal ke liye".

❧❧❧

TEN
RAISING DAUGHTERS

Of course, daughters are a blessing for the house but raising daughters is also a huge responsibility on the parents. In this society filled with hatred, lust, guilt, and evil eye, one has to worry for daughters many times more than sons. Islam has always given a great status and honor to daughters, Rasulullah Sallallahu Alaihi wa Aalihi wa Sallam considered and declared daughters to be the mercy for the house in that period, blessing for the parents. In an era when the girls were buried alive as soon as they were born, Islam gave such an honour to woman that somewhere it is proclaimed that heaven lies beneath the steps of a mother, sometimes it called a sister a companion of joy and sorrow, a wife as a partner in life, a daughter as a mercy and a daughter-in-law the beauty of the house. Islam has always given woman an honorary status in every way.

I don't like to talk one-sidedly, so I will also state this fact openly that even though Islam has given great honour to women, but the men of our community left behind the teachings of the Qur'an and Ahlebait Alaihimusallam, and started taking decisions on their own and even started making their own patrons and lobbying them. Even the so-called Muslims and all the worldly men did not give women the due respect which she deserved.

Almost every religion in this world has asserted the great status of women, but despite this, molestation, rape, exploitation of girls is becoming common day by day in our society. Girls are still considered a burden; they are not given their due share of rights and are considered inferior. Islam advises to pay more attention and labour on the upbringing, education and training of daughters, because it is through the daughters only that true religion and goodness travel through the generations and the daughter becomes a mercy and adornment for two households.

Many girls of our community are fleeing with boys of another caste. According to me, there is no boundary between love and friendship, but it is also true that a person who believes in Allah falls in love with a person of the same belief. There are three things worth considering here. The first thing is that the parents could not give their children the right education and upbringing. Secondly, they fail to develop in their children the understanding of truth, the difference between halal and haram (permissible and non permissible), right and wrong, truth and falsehood. And the third thing is that our clerics called people like Yazid, Yazid's father, Marwan, Mughira as Raziyallah, and then the question very likely to arise is that which woman would like to live with Muslims who consider Yazid's father as their role model?

I have spoken to many Muslims and found that there are people who believe that Muhammad Rasullulah Sallallahu Alaihe wa Aalihi wa Sallam is the founder of Islam as taught in our schools while Muhammad Sallallahu Alaihe wa Aalihi wa Sallam is in actual the last Messenger of Allah and the last prophet of Islam.

Similarly, the Quran is not the first but the last book of Islam which has come for the entire mankind, and many creatures are benefiting from it. So my people! Men who do not know the basics of their own religion, what can we expect them to teach their wives and children? Save your girls from such beasts who are ruining their religion and faith and I am not saying that you need to fight the bad and cunning people in the community to save the girls rather you just need to raise your children in the right way within the four walls of your home.If your upbringing and education proves effective and your children are able to implement that training or education, then Insha Allah, your children will remain steadfast on the right path and even in this bad situation will be able to protect themselves.

Take care of your daughter, educate her, teach her Haqq Deen, explain to her about halal and haram, explain about the evils spread in society, warn her against the wrong and nefarious intentions of boys, explain them against the analogy of those beasts who possess lust in the name of love. I repeat that if you connect your children with the Quran and Ahlebait Alaihimusallam, they will automatically be guided to the right path.There are millions of evils spread in the world but the main cause of all of them is the same, "Not holding on to the Quran and Ahlebait Alaihimusallam", and the cure for all these evils is also the same, "Holding on to the Quran and Ahlebait". Allahumma Salle Ala Muhammad Wa Ala Aale Muhammad.

"Miri beti, Miri jaanaa
Tumhe sab yaad to hoga
Bohot pehle bohot pehle
Jawani ka tha jab aalam
Mire baazu mein taaqat thi
Mire seene mein himmat thi

Unhe ayyaam mein ik din
Miri aagosh-e-ulfat mein
Kisi ne la ke rakha tha
Tmhara phool sa chehra
Badan be-intiha naazuk
Mire in sakht haathon mein
Ajab narmi si aayi thi
Miri is aankh ne boo se liye the aur royi thi
Mujhe to yaad hai sab kuch
Tumhe bhi yaad to hoga
Naye kapde khilone,doodh ki botal khareedi thi
Bohot bechain hota tha jo tum raaton ko roti thi
Chali thi apne pairon par jo tum pehle-pahal beta
Mujhe aisa laga tha chal padi dil ki mire dhadkan
Qadam do chaar le kar tum jo ik-dam ladkhadayi thi
Miri saansein mire seene ke andar thartharayi thi
Miri godi mein rafta rafta din guzra kiye aur tum
Na jaane sote sote mere seene par jawani tak
Miri jaan aaj aayi ho
Tumhein mujh se shikaayat hai
Ki main ne sakhtiyaan ki hain
Mire wo sakhtiyaan tum ko bohot ranjoor karati thi
Mujhe bhi ranj hota tha
magar thi tarbiyat laazim
Tumhe saanche mein dhalana tha
Tabiyat ko badalna tha
Tumhen sab yaad to hoga
Miri beti mire baazu mein wo quwat nahi baaki
Tumhari har khushi ki hai zamaanat dhadakne meri
Magar ik mashwara sun lo
Ki ab sab bhool jao tum
Naye rishte banao tum
hamara saath chhootega
Naye rishton ke meri jaan masail kam nahin honge
Magar tab ham nahin honge

Akeli jaan hogi tum
Faqat wo tarbiyat hogi
Jo maine sakhtiyaan kar ke
Tumhare dil mein daali hai
Wo tum ko yaad to hogi
Sabaq sab yaad to hoga".

❧❧❧

ELEVEN

RIGHTS OF A DAUGHTER

Rasulullah Sallallahu Alaihe wa Alaihi Wa Sallam stated daughters as a mercy. His progeny was carried further by his daughter only. Rasulullah Sallallahu Alaihe wa Aalihi Wasallam mentioned his daughter to be the leader of all the heavenly women and in the form of his inheritance, Zameen-e-Fadaq (Land of Fadak) was also given by Him to his daughter, but the Ummah took away that land of Fadaq from Bibi Fatima Salamullah Alaiha. In front of the first caliph made by the ummah, daughter of Prophet Muhammad! rose as the first woman lawyer but alas! The women of the nation did not support Fatima Salamullah Alaiha and even today they mention others more than the Prophet's daughter and later complain that the society is oppressing us, we are not getting our rights and so on.

First of all, I want to say to the sisters and daughters of our society that you should cease saying that a man does wrong with a woman, because the mother-in-law who troubles the daughter-in-law is also a woman, a sister-in-law agitating another is also a woman.The daughter-in-law who disrespects the mother-in-law is also a woman and the sister-in-law who dislikes and hates another is also a woman. Rituals like dowry, offerings, jewels, etc and later complaining about the reciepts are carried on as tradition by women only. The ever quarreling sister in laws are none but women only.

So the sister-daughters of the Ummah! Give good upbringing to your children, if Allah has given you a son, then make him a good person. If a man does not respect a woman, does not pay her due rights, then women (mothers) should pay heed to their upbringing and try fixing it as soon as possible.

I also appeal to the men of our society to give their daughter a share in their inheritance as prescribed by Islam law. Father should fulfill the rights of daughters, sons should fulfill the rights of their mothers, brothers should fulfill the rights of their sisters and husbands should fulfill the rights of their wives. I will say a bitter thing here, but this is a fact that whenever a man tries to pay the due rightsto a woman, it is often the woman who puts a constraint. For example, if a son wants to do something for his mother and sister, this becomes troublesome for his wife, and if a husband wants to do something for his wife, then it's the vice versa. So my brothers! Keep paying all the rights to my sisters and daughters! You should not be a hindrance in the payment of someone's rights. A woman should support a woman, but the opposite is mostly seen in the society.

Parents are generally bound by a daughter's hundreds of rights both big and small but all those rights come within these four rights. The first right of a daughter on her parents is that she should be given the right education and upbringing, the the second one is that she should be taught to differentiate between halal and haram, right and wrong, truth and falsehood that is,basic worldly knowledge must be taught. The third right is that she should be married to a worthy and pious man, and the fourth one is that she should be paid her rights i.e. her share in the inheritance/property.

If for some reason, a father has not been able to give the rightful share to his daughter or has left this world without writing a will or due to negligence has divided his inheritance only among the sons, then remember, that in the Quran, Allah Rab Ul Izzat has himself explained how to divide the inheritance, Rasulullah Sallallahu Alaihe Wa Alaihi Wa Sallam has explained the same in detail and now no Muslim man or woman has the right to make decisions according to their own desire in this matter, therefore a daughter's right cannot be usurped. Fathers give your daughter's their share, if he is not able to give it then brothers should fulfill this duty and remember that whoever tries to usurp the rights of a daughter or sister will buy for himself the Hellfire on the doomsday. Illa Masha'Allah.

"Main bhi duniya ki tarah jeene ka haq maangti hun,
Isko gaddari ka ailaan na samajha jaye,
   Ab to bete bhi chale jaate hain ho kar rukhsat,
Sirf beti ko hi mehmaan na samajha jaye".

ᰔᰔᰔ

TWELVE

DIFFERENCE BETWEEN HALAL AND HARAM

As I have mentioned earlier, it is a duty for every parent to give their child at least enough knowledge so that the child learns to distinguish between Halal and Haram i.e permissible and non permissible. I believe that if parents connect their children with the Quran and Ahlebait Alaihissalam and teach them to distinguish between halal and haram, then the child will gradually but surely learn to follow the right path by itself.

Today it is often found in our society, that the boys of our community marry polytheist women and boast that they have connected so-and-so with Islam, this is nothing but open ignorance and some girls are also fleeing away with polytheist men because their parents and siblings fail to serve them the true Islam. Even though Mutaah (temporary marriage) with Ahle Kitab (People of the Book) is permissible or some ulema (scholars) also permit Nikah (Marriage) with them , but considering the current scenario, this should also be avoided.By the way, I believe that love and friendship cannot be divided, this feeling knows no boundaries of the country, caste, religion etc. but still considering the present situation, the young boys and girls of our community should avoid such marriages. The foremost thing is that marriage of a monotheist to a polytheist is impossible and the second thing is that when there lays a danger of spoiling the environment because of your marriage, what else would such an act be except ignorance?

Most of the boys and girls who flee with people of different caste, their parents have often been found to be oblivious to religion. Many times it can also happen that the children of good, pious, charitable parents also turn out to be spoiled and ignorant, but this is very rare. When parents themselves do not know or understand Deen (religion), how will they teach the same to their children? After the demise of the Prophet, the Ummah of Muhammad Sallallahu Alaihe wa Aalihi wa Sallam soon forgot his commands and started following the rulers they had elected. Since then until today, whatever corruption has spread in the community has only one root cause and that is not holding onto the Quran and Ahlebayt Alaihimusallam and the cure is also the same, "Hold the Qur'an and Ahlebayt, this is the only way to the truth and success."

The followers of Ali Alaihissalam should try to marry only among the people having the faith, I do not intend to say that marriage is not permissible in other sects, infact marriage between a shia and a sunni is also cent percent permissible but if there arises any dispute between the two related to their respective belief, apart from personal ones, then the life of the husband and wife will be wasted in arguments and fighting and they will ultimately remain oblivious to the correct upbringing of their children. In view of the current situation, it is better to build kinship among people of the same faith. So, my loved ones, when you teach your children to distinguish between halal and haram, try to make them understand the same in matters of relationships and love too.

In the times to come, your children will either grow up to be freelancers or get a job or will have their own setups, that mean the children of today are the future of tomorrow. So teach your children honesty, make them avoid Haram. It is not only haram to earn money in a wrong way, but it is also haram not to do one's work properly with due effort. It is also wrong to make excessive undue profits, and it is also illicit to sell bad goods by deception.

"Halaal rizq ka matlab kisaan se pucho,
Paseena ban ke badan se lahu nikalta hai".

My loved ones! Whether it is about sustenance, job or business, relationships or hundreds of daily tasks, one has to keep in mind the understanding of right and wrong, halal-haram, legal and illegal, just and unjust at every step and needs to save oneself from evil while remaining steadfast on righteousness. It seems very difficult to even think that how to save oneself in this age full of devilry and in a spoiled society, but believe me; holding on to the Quran and Ahlebait Alaihimussalam makes this journey very easy.

"Sau jaan se fida hun Mohammad ke naam par,
Jinhone bataaya farq Haraam o halaal ka".

May Allah Rabb ul Izzat save us all and our progeny from Haram. Allahu Akbar Kaseeran Kaseera. Allahumma Salle Ala Muhammad wa Ala Aale Muhammad.

ʔʔʔ

THIRTEEN

SPREADING THE SUNNAH OF MARRIAGE

This rapidly changing world and the changing thought process of the society has harmed the entire ummah and has slowly destroyed people's faith, people have left the Quran and Ahlebait Alaihissalam, the real religion has been replaced by Takhliqi(false) religion. However, I believe that one of the deeds that have caused the most damage to our Ummah is, "Not getting married at the right time."

I myself contemplated on this during my school and college days that today children get involved in illicit (haram) relationships from the age of 13-14 years and by the time they reach the age of 20-22 years, they become addicted to such relationships. In our country, the minimum age of marriage is 18 years for a girl and 21 years for a boy and marrying under this age is considered a crime, but the bitter truth is that most of the youngsters in our country and around the world get involved in illicit relationships from the age of 13-14 itself.

There are many reasons behind this, so I don't think it is right to highlight any one of them and cover the rest, so I am stating the seven main reasons. One reason is that people lack the knowledge of religion, the second reason is that parents are oblivious to fulfilling this important Sunnah for their children, the third reason is that our society has made marriage difficult and adultery common. The fourth reason is poverty and the fifth is unreasonable rituals and customs in the process of marriage. The sixth reason is that this society has taken away the rights of both boys and girls. Parents should try to know from their children about the kind of person they want to live with and the way of life they want or if the children tell them about their choice, then think on it but the reverse happens. Parents find a person of their own choice and get their children married; this is why youngsters dislike marriage. And the seventh and most important reason is distancing oneself from Ahlebait Alaihimussalam.

I would like to say one more thing, if your children tell you about their choice for marriage then do consider it.Remember that relationships can turn out to be good or bad, either they are chosen by you or by your children. One of the bitter truths of this society is that if the parents fix a match for their children and the boy or girl turns out to be bad, then they console their children by saying,"It was written in fate, be patient and try to make everything better." But at the same time, if the children choose their partner and then the boy or the girl turns out to be bad, then all the accountability and blame is labelled on the children and it is said to them, "You are suffering because of your own choice of marriage", etc.

Halal is always better than Haraam, if your children are addicted to illicit relationships from their school and college days then you should teach them Haqq,so that they can avoid Haram and as soon as they reach the legal age of marriage,marry them as per sunnah and give them a halal relationship. In our community, Nikah (Marriage) should be made so easy that adultery becomes difficult, i.e. if a boy and a girl think to commit a haraam deed it should seem difficult to them and Nikah easy. Some people say that first one should achieve and become something and then get married,I too agree with this but only when it saves us from Haraam. If one can study and build a career while living in a haram relationship, then similar things can be done while living in a halal one. Pretentiousness (Show-off) has become common in our society, unwanted rituals and customs have made their place in the society, the implementation of Deen and Shariah (Islamic law) has been left to no avail. Extravagant spending has become common in weddings. We need to save ourselves and the community from all these frivolous activities, rituals and customs. Make the process of marriage simple.The rich Muslims of the society should marry their sons to the girls of the poor Muslim and the wealthy Saadats should also marry and build relationships with the poor Sadaats, indeed this is the best practice.

At the time of marriage, boys should opt for a humble, polite, virtuous, knowledgeable, skilled girl for themselves, even if she is not very beautiful and charming and girls should prefer a humble, virtuous, worthy, knowledgeable, skilled boy. Don't waste your life chasing someone who is wealthier but lacks the knowledge of deen (religion). We need to correct and upgrade the standard of our thinking as well.

"Amal mein baaki Nabi ka farmaan hona chahiye,
   Nikaah, Zina ke nisbat, aasaan hona chahiye"

My loved ones! We also have to end this plague of dowry because poor parents mostly delay their daughter's marriage because they are neither capable to give dowry nor have enough money to feed, give gifts and make arrangements for the wedding procession. Gradually this plague became widespread and now the situation is such that about 6-8 thousand cases of murder and deaths are registered every year because of the evil of dowry system and many cases even go unregistered, only Allah knows about the actual figure.

"Baap bojh dhhota tha, kya jahez de pata,
Isliye wo shahzadi aaj tak kunwari hai".

My loved ones! There is still time, keep trying to improve your society and community as soon as possible and do remember, if you want to change the world, change has to begin with you, first improvise yourself, then your family members, then your relatives, then your neighbours and friends and slowly and steadily this change begins to take place in the whole world. If the children and youth of the community come forward, then though difficult but bringing the change is not impossible.

ᕤᕤᕤ

FOURTEEN

RELATIVES OR DEVILS

I believe that one of the best blessings that Allah Rabb ul Izzat has given us is relationships, but unfortunately people have filled relationships with so much bullying, greed, envy and evils that now relatives and the devils seem no different. The role of relatives is to support one another in their times of distress, problems and difficult situations, but on the contrary, relatives are seen making fun of them in such situations and sympathy and support seem distant things.

Allah has also commanded in the Quran and Muhammad and Aaal-e Muhammad Sallallahu Alaihe wa Alihi wa Sallam has also instructed to avoid breaking relationships, do not violate rights in relationships, and to support each other. Relatives are the ones who are meant to stand together in times of happiness and sorrow, but unfortunately people did not pay heed to the instructions of their own God, Prophet and Ahlebait Alaihimusallam and went on worsening the relationships.

Today, the situation of the community is such that brothers are usurping the rights of brothers, brothers are violating the rights of their own sisters, they are creating problems for each other and their hearts are filled with envy, resentment and jealousy.

"Rishton ki daldal se kaise niklenge,
Har saazish ke piche apne niklenge."

Now the situation is that a good man can maintain a relationship only as long as he remains silent on the bullying, evils and encroachments of the relatives, and as soon as he tries to raise his voice for his rights, the relations end automatically. I have seen many such people in this community, who discuss religion day and night, talk about honesty, equity and justice, and if we look into their own lives, it is found that they themselves have usurped the shares of their own brothers or sisters. How can anyone snatch away from someone the share which has been fixed in Shariah by Allah and his Messenger?

If a person succeeds in life, it becomes a source of pain for the relatives, if someone's child starts studying well, the relatives start getting envious, if someone's progresses in any work, relatives are filled with malice against them, on the other hand if a person is ruined, the relatives feel a kind of peace and happiness. Some relatives hide this satanic happiness in their hearts, but some relatives go beyond the limit, and start taunting, and speaking ill and start revealing their true faces.

There are many reasons for the breakdown of relationships, but one of the main reasons is backbiting and slandering. In people, especially in women, this quality is mostly found that they spread rumours from here to there, and gossip and then sourness is created in people's hearts.Another thing that should be kept in mind is that often when people are spreading the word from here to there, they exaggerate things from their side, which in common parlance is called embellishing statements or sometimes people say the same thing but in such a way which changes the perception of the entire matter. However, what is the need of gossip and backbiting? My loved ones! Avoid this disease that eats relationships like termites.

Snitching is one of the worst habits found in humans. Gossip is not just that if you get to know something about someone, then you speak ill of him behind his back. But also, if a person swears and confesses about his own bad habit or vices, you should not repeat any of his words again. I think it is important to tell one more thing here because some of our clerics, use one of the sayings as a shield to defend some traitors of our religion, that is "to disclose the mistakes, mischiefs and misbehaviours of any historical figure is also snitching" but the fact is telling about the cruelty of an oppressor is not gossip. Likewise, when we investigate the hadiths as a seeker of knowledge, then if we do not consider a narrator to be credible, then the hadith of his statement can be doubted. The question here is not about the hadith but about the truthfulness of the person who narrated the hadith, and even while reading historical events, if the character of a person appears to be duplicitous or he appears to be a traitor and you also have arguments, then you can express your opinion for that person as well.

In the current era, if you find someone is trying to harm others or you think that you can save any of your loved ones from being a victim of fraud, bullying, deception, and then warning them is not a bad thing.Another thing that comes to mind is that I have often seen people gossiping by mispercieving something that did not even happen or something that is suspected and attribute it to a particular person. For example, a marriage took place in someone's house and a reception feast was arranged, if one of those who received the invitation could not attend the feast, some people without knowing the reason start saying, so-and-so did not come on purpose, or has pride, or is envious and so on. In my view, talking like this is similar to thinking of oneself as God, so this should be avoided at all costs.

"Sabhi rishton ke darwaze muqaffal ho rahe hain,
Hamaare beech jo raste the, daldal ho rahe hain."

Mother and daughter in laws or sister in laws are such relationships in which people from two different families meet and stay with each other but one should avoid fighting and arguments and even if some sort of quarrel takes place then do not keep estrangements.The daughter-in-law should treat her mother and father in laws like her own parents and they should also try to give the same respect and love to their daughter-in-law that they want for their daughter. Husband and wife should also build a strong understanding of 'forgive and forget' between each other. The teaching of Ahlebayt Alaihimusallam is that real love between a husband and wife is not limited to sexual pleasure and companionship, but real love is to pardon and forgive each other's faults.

My dear ones! Every relationship has its own rights and violation of rights is a big sin. Remember that Allah forgives shortfalls in Huquq-ul-Allah(duties towards Allah)but mistakes made in Huquq-ul-Ibad(The rights and duties of one soul over another) cannot be escaped without being punished, and usurping the rights of relatives is also considered as not fulfilling Huquq-ul-Ibad.If we contemplate on the teachings of our Aaimma e Ahlebait Alaihimusallam, we will find that about 70%-80% of the evils spread in relationships in the Ummah will end only if we do not do violate each other's rights.

• 58 •

May Allah Rabb ul Izzat make us all doers rather than hearers. Allahu Akbar Kaseeran Kaseera. Allahumma Salle Ala Muhammad wa Ala Aale Muhammad.

"Taalluq kirchhiyon ki shakl mein bikhra to hai phir bhi,
Shikasta aaino ko jod dena chaahte hain ham".

❧❧❧

FIFTEEN

DETERIORATION OF THE SOCIETY

Allah's Messenger Muhammad Sallalahu Alaihi Wa Alaihi Wassalam commanded the Ummah to hold on to the Quran and Ahlebait Alaihimusallam. The beloved of Allah had also given a guarantee that as long as the ummah holds on to these two important things i.e. the Quran and the AhleBayt, it will never go astray. But unfortunately soon after the demise of the Prophet, the Ummah refused and rejected to accept his sayings and were misled. This fallacy is increasing day by day and the society is getting worse.I repeat one thing again and again, there is only one way to reach Allah, to be successful, to please God and that is to hold on to the Quran and the Ahle Bayt. My loved ones! Nothing will improve until the ummah takes hold of the Quran and Ahle Bayt Alaihimusallam.

In the Ummah, many defects are found at every step, but the biggest deteriorations are - distance from the Quran and Ahlebait, violation of rights, lack of education, delay in marriage, backbiting, fornication, lying, hiding the truth, fear of death, sectarianism, personalism, dowry, extravagance, promiscuity, adultery, following the ways of Jews and Christians, etc. Even if we consider and improve only these 14-15 things, we can bring about a huge change in our community. Rather, I even say that 70% to 80% of the damage can be mended only by correcting one act and that is, we should stop usurping and violating each other's rights.

"Ye la-ilaaj marz hai, rishton ko khatm karta hai,
Haq-talfi ne na jaane kitne gharon ko toda hai".

The widespread promiscuity and adultery has also created a mess in the community. Young men roaming day and night on the roads and lanes and girls promoting indecency in the name of zeal and modernity have caused a lot of harm to the society and community. Today there are a lot of apps like Facebook, YouTube, Tiktok, Instagram etc. on which young boys and girls are seen dancing and performing mujra. When these young boys and girls of today will get married tomorrow and become parents, what education and training will they be able to give to their children?

It is a matter of great shame, but I am seeing that Muslim young men too are now engaged in consumption of alcohol, drugs and gambling and are ruining themselves which means that the commands which were given by Allah, they could not abide by them rather things, which have been declared haram, they are leaving no stone unturned to fulfill them. Especially since the start of IPL, gambling in the name of cricket has become very common and people also bet amongst each other. And gambling-related ads are also openly circulated on TV's and social media platforms and big celebrities are seen promoting them.

In our society, people think that it is only the responsibility of the children to fulfill the rights of the parents; only the wife has the responsibility of managing the house, only the daughter-in-law has the responsibility to understand the in-laws, etc., but the reality is the opposite. In fact, all of us have been obliged to pay heed to each other's rights but in one way or the other all of us are violating someone's rights knowingly or unknowingly. Children have rights over their parents; parents have rights over their children too. Husband-wife, brothers-sisters, relatives, even neighbours and the whole Ummah, even every creature has some rights on you, which must be fulfilled.

Let's not think so far for the moment because today hundreds of evils are flourishing amidst parents-children, mother and daughter in laws, husband-wife, siblings and the distance continues even in close relationships. I have even seen that even on the day of Eid, one brother is not ready to meet and embrace his own brother. May Allah have mercy on us. My loved ones! Repent from the sin of violating rights and give your loved ones their share and fulfill your responsibilities.

"Huquq ul khuda hain baad mein, Pehle hain huquq ul ibaad,
Huquq kar ada gar chahta ho tu apni magfirat".

A plague spread in the society which has ruined it is dowry. Try to eradicate the dowry system completely and start this noble work from your own home. Try to stop the various ignorant rituals prevalent in the name of marriage. The advantage of this would be that even a poor father would be able to get his daughter married easily and bad deeds like fornication (Zina) would also stop to a great extent. As adultery decreases, gradually indecency, slander, will also go on decreasing and this will bring a massive change in the society.

Extravagant spending and showoff, these are also big calamities that lead to the destruction of society, whether it is the occasion of marriage or any function, there is also a lot of showoff and extravagant spending. Infact people nowadays, have associated the obligation of Hajj, Qurbani in Eid to Nazar, Niyaz, Fatiha and other form of worships with showoff. People have started performing these acts not to please Allah but to prove their relatives-neighbours low and themselves super-rich and thus waste money instead. My loved ones! Save yourself from these ignorant deeds and live your life for the sake of pleasing Allah.

My dear ones! Not being able to give proper upbringing and education to your children is also an important reason for the deterioration of the society. Education gives the child the ability and skill to learn, live, earn, become something and achieve something in this world, and through proper upbringing the child learns how to live a life with morality, honesty, virtues while remaining steadfast on the path of religion and ultimately live a life so as to please Allah. Illa Masha'Allah.

"Kyun qaum baithi hai, jahaalat ke andhere mein
Taaleem o tarbiyat se badalta hai muashra".

As I have mentioned earlier in this topic that gossip, slander, lies, which are often spread by relatives and neighbors in a community, play an important role in breaking and spoiling relationships. At the same time, being envious and jealous of each other also becomes the root cause of destruction and damage. We should try to be supportive of our relatives and neighbours in their happiness and sorrow, if we see someone in distress, we should try to support them, instead of making fun of them which is surely as if following the path of evil. Don't laugh at someone's bad times and circumstances because neither the time remains the same nor the circumstances of one person, worse times can also come upon you, so keep fearing your Lord and keep repenting.

Nowadays, evil eye, black magic, satanic knowledge, sorcery, etc. are also increasing in the community. Let me tell you one more thing here that out of 100 people who claim that someone has done black magic on them, 99 of them have only an illusion and only one or two such case remains, in which it has actually been done. Therefore, to save people from superstition and getting psychologically ill, it is often said that there is no such things as evil eye, black magic, etc. although those who think themselves to be highly educated also use terms like positive energy, negative energy, positive vibes, negative vibes. My dear ones, I will not write much about witchcraft and black magic, I will just say that going to devils with the intention of ruining someone else's life or harming someone, will ruin both your world and the hereafter. Now the question is of that person on whom you have wanted to activate such black magics, so if Allah wills, he will be saved because devilish thing are not so powerful that it cannot be reversed by Allah's scriptures.

Now let's talk about evil eye, so my loved ones! There are two types of glances, good glances and bad glances, but you must have heard only about the evil glances or evil eye because we tend to believe that the people can only put evil eyes on others which is colloquially called as casting an evil eye on others, but we have ever thought that if the evil eye can be destructive and it can spoil the health or work of a person, then there must be a good eye too. For example, if you look at the history, you will find that if our Prophet, Wali, Imam, Saints give a glance at someone, that person changes from worse to best, from sinner to pious, his works get accomplished, health improves and so on. So have we ever thought that what is this? Actually, the kind of people we are and the kind of thinking and determination we have when we look at someone that shows the effect. If we are bad people and look upon someone with bad intentions and motives then it will surely have a bad effect.On the contrary if we pious and look at someone with good intentions then it will ultimately have a good effect on him. Always keep a good eye on others and keep trying to make yourself the best and earn the world and the hereafter instead of working hard to destroy others.

Lying and concealing the truth also became a major reason for the destruction of our society and the bitter truth is that our clerics are found at the forefront of lying and concealing the truth. Instead it should have happened that our clerics and scholars should speak the truth and lead the Ummah towards the truth, but in the process of usurping the rights of Ahlebait of the Prophet, most of the clerics (maulvis) became followers of Satan.

Now the question arises that what has been the effect of concealing the rights of Ahlebait Alaihimusallam on the Ummah? It so happened that even today people are supporting those people by calling them Sahaba who spent their entire life persecuting and oppressing the progeny of our Prophet and harming the Deen. On the other hand, if the clerics had told the truth and awaken people, they would have been advocating and following Ahlebait Alaihimusallam, and the door of Ahlebait is that lyceum which transforms man into human and unites him with God.

Sectarianism has also played an important role in ruining the community and the clerics have also done the diabolical work of misleading people from the truth and turning them towards sectarianism. People are far from the right path and they are busy thinking that their sect is only right and they are engaged in following their own sect instead of Islam. They are giving preference to their sectarian books instead of Quran. The clerics have opened their shops for the battle of donations and the naive Ummats are fighting with each other, while the battle is more about donations than faith.

Alas! When a person sinks into sectarianism, he automatically starts to do personalism. When the madness of sectarianism crosses its limits, then these sectarians start to prove that the maulvis and pirs of their sect are the most honourable and try to prove the masters of other sects are infidels (Kafirs). They prefer to follow their clerics instead of the commands and teachings of Allah, Rasullulah and Ahlebayt and fill the society with evils.

(Sallalahu Alaihi Wa Aalihi Wassalam)

Another reason for the deterioration in the society is the fear of death. Yes! Earlier, Muslims used to be afraid of Allah alone and longed for martyrdom, but now the situation has reversed, now the Muslim are also inclined towards worldliness and is afraid of dying. We need to remove the fear of death from our hearts and also remove cowardice. Even if hundreds of people stand against us, we need to face them with courage, wisdom and bravery and for this it is important that we recite the event of Karbala to our offsprings and connect them to the Quran and Ahlebait.

It is also the ignorance of the Muslims that they have abandoned the teachings of their Prophet (Sallalahu Alaihi Wa Aalihi Wassalam) and have chosen to follow the ways of Jews, Hindus and Christians. Today, whether it is dress, lifestyle, manners or life, we do not advocate Islam, Quran or Ahlebait, but others and move away from our own culture, civilization, religion, law (Shariat) and live life according to others. If we only think about our life, apart from our belief and faith, we will find that there is no difference between us and others.

• 66 •

May Allah Rabb ul Izzat make us all doers more than speakers and listeners. Allahu Akbar Allahu Khabeer, Allahu Rahman, Allahu Rahim.

"Vaz mein tum ho Nasaara to tamaddun mein Hunood,
    Ye musalmaan hain jinhedekh ke sharmaye Yahood".

ᗝᗝᗝ

SIXTEEN

SAADATS IN THE SOCIETY

Now let's talk about the responsibilities of a Saadat in the society and what should a Saadat do to stop the spread of corruption in the community? So my Saadat brothers, sisters and elders,first of all you need to understand that you are the progeny of Rasulullah, children of Batool, the offspring of Maula Ali Alaihissalam i.e. you are a member of the family of Hasnain Karimain and your first responsibility is to defend Tawheed, Rasalat, Wilayat, Imamat and Haqq-e-Fatima Salamullah Alaiha and spread the truth.

The second and most important responsibility of a Saadat is to give up sectarianism, give up personalism and unite on one faith. Today a Saadat also calls himself Shia, Sunni, Barelvi, Deobandi, Ahle-Hadith, Hanafi, Shafa'i, Maliki, Hambali etc. Infact, I have seen some Saadats associated with Barelvi sect arguing to prove Hazrat Abu Talib as a disbeliever, it is not that they are doing this because they are fake Saadat, but the fact is that if a poisonous snake bites, a person will die whether he is a Saadat or non Saadat it does not matter. Similarly, when the poison of a cleric spreads, along with the non-Saadats, the Saadats also fall under its grip, those who do not have much knowledge or are heedless of religion or are engaged in sectarianism and personalism. So my Saadat brothers and sisters! You should unite at one point i.e. Dar e Ahlebait Alaihimusallam, without stumbling here and here.

"Koi Abuzar, koi Qambar, koi Salman banta hai,
Dar e Zahra par aakar aadmi, Insaan banta hai".

The third responsibility of the Saadats is that they should free themselves from the constraint of sects and read and understand each and every sect and contemplate on them. Investigate the truth yourself and after accepting it, work hard to convey the truth to others. Truth remains truth even if it is against our own beliefs and wrong is wrong even if it is part of the teachings of the religious leaders of our sects. So my loved ones! If you are Saadat or lovers and followers of Ahlebait Alaihimussalam, you should keep spreading the truth every moment, every second.

Allah Rab-ul-Izzat has also explained his words in the Quran by giving examples and therefore I think that anything explained by giving examples can be easily understood and when there are only spoils and deterioration all around in the community, then It becomes necessary that we ourselves, being Saadats, Aal-e-Rasool, should come forward to stop every evil spread in the society. I have written in detail in the previous topic that what evils have spread in the community, so instead of repeating them, I will try to tell what the Saadats should do.

So my dear Saadat brothers and sisters! You should come forward and raise your voice against the ridiculous rituals and customs and start it with your own self. Dowry system should be stopped, ignorance happening in the name of marriages should be stopped.

Nikah should be done with simplicity, business should be done honestly, truth should be spread, one should stay away from personalism and sectarianism and set yourself as an example. One should present himself as such an example through which the Ummah can take guidance.

Ahle Saadat should come forward for the assistance of Imam Mehdi, learn and spread knowledge, convey the truth to the people, especially the oppression suffered by Ahlebait, spread the rights of Zahra, Ali, Hasan and Hussain Alaihissalam. Come forward to remove all the evils and malpractices done in the name of religion and first of all explain by presenting yourself as an example through your actions and words. You have to present yourself as an ideal as a Saadat and progeny of Ahlebait Alaihimussalam.

All the Saadats and followers of Ahlebait Alaihimussalam should put aside and pay Khums so that even those Saadats who are financially weak can become strong. Financially strong wealthy saadats should bring daughters of poor saadat families as daughters-in-law. While getting married, give more importance to character, personality and manners rather than outward appearance. Bring such a life partner who can fill your children's heart with Quran and Ahlebait Alaihimussalam in such a way that the aim of the child's life becomes Karbala and Nusrat-e-Imam.

It is also a fact that this Ummah started torturing our Prophet's progeny soon after his demise. Those who should have been made to sit on the pulpits, were abused from the pulpits and since then till today efforts are being made to keep the Saadats below the pulpits. Anyways, we are the lovers of that Meesam-e-Tammar who recited Khutba making his death place as his pulpit and spread the love of Ali Alaihissalam. So my loved ones! First improve yourself, then start rectifying things and spreading truth from your own home, then extend it to your relatives, family members and neighbours. Our first effort should be that we should try to bring all the Saadats on one platform and our second effort should be to bring all the lovers of Ahlebait Alaihimussalam along with us.

Many people often ask me that when you talk about unity, why do you call Yazid's father bad when a large section of Ahle Sunnah are convinced of his companionship. So my loved ones! We do not speak ill of anyone, but only tell their truth. We want unity but we want it on the basis of truth. If the condition of being united is that we pledge allegiance to falsehood, then it was unacceptable to us yesterday and it is still unacceptable to us even today.As for the question of unity of the Ummah, surely we always look for the return of "Hurr" and not "Hurmala". The ummah that could not unite on the call of Hussain Ibn Ali, Sibt e Rasool, hiw can it unite on our and your call? We are working hard for the Hurr of this age. Hurmala was a Yazidi once and forever.

My loved ones! A child's training starts from the mother's womb itself but we think because of lack of knowledge that first the child will be 7-10 or 13 years old, then he will learn something by taking training and education. All the saadat and lovers of Panjatan Pak, brothers and sisters should pay special attention to the education of their children because this will become the main reason for change. The darkness of ignorance can only be dispelled by the light of knowledge.If you look at the ignorant people who are caught up in sectarianism, you will find that they have no knowledge or only very little knowledge of a particular sect.

So my dear brothers, sisters! Start the hard work for Deen from today and start the hard work of bringing people to the door of

Ahlebayt Alaihimusallam, i.e. away from evil and bring them closer to the truth, and first of all, invite those Sadat who due to lack of knowledge or due to negligence or due to the cleric's delusions, are in the grip of different sects and are engaged in popularizing their cleric's belief.

Akbar Kaseeran Kaseera. Allahumma Salle Ala Muhammad wa Ala Aale Muhammad.

"Muttahid ho to badal daalo duniya ka nizaam,
Muntashir ho to maro, shor machaate kyun ho?"

༺༺༺

SEVENTEEN
FEAR OF DEATH

It is the fear of death that has turned our people into cowards and has consumed the minds of the youth. We belong to a community that cherishes martyrdom, does not fear death but only one Lord. In earlier times, when the mothers of our community used to raise her children, she would fill the heart of her child with the spirit of martyrdom to such an extent that the children ultimately grew up to be courageous. The youth of the community should used to dedicate their lives to Allah and wished for martyrdom while living in this world.

My loved ones! Living in this world, everything in your life is uncertain except death. For example, will you be sick or healthy, will you earn more money or less, where will you get married, will you get a job or not, will your business work or not, infact every moment, every second, every little thing. is uncertain. But only death is certain.I always say that death is an open secret, open because it is bound to come and secret because when, where, how, under what circumstances death will come is a secret. Now if death is inevitable then what will be the best way of death? Death in illness and suffering or death for the sake of God, Martyrdom. Do contemplate on this.

"Har Musalmaan rag-e-baatil ke liye nashtar tha,
Uske aaina-e-hasti mein amal jauhar tha,
Jo bharosa tha use quwat-e-baazoo par tha ,
Hai tumhein maut ka dar, usko khuda ka dar tha".

In fact, the reality is that the world has settled in our hearts and we have become heedless towards religion. We have become so engrossed in the world that we have forgotten the ultimate reality of life i.e. death, whereas we should have stood for the right, the truth, the oppressed and pleased our Lord by following the footsteps of Hasnain Kariman. My loved ones! When life is in danger, it should be saved by giving charity, but when religion and faith are in danger, it should be saved by sacrificing one's life.

Martyrdom does not mean that we unnecessarily get entangled with people and start fighting, but it definitely means that we should not have any fear from the enemies; we need not live like a jackal for hundred days, but like a lion for one day. Be an attack on the dignity of any sister or daughter or we are stopped from following our religion. If any victim is being oppressed or someone's rights are being denied, we should raise our voice. Instead of fighting with our opponent first we should try for reconciliation, but if he is inclined on war, then the war should also be fought with courage.

"Hum aman chahte hain magar, Zulm ke khilaaf
Gar jung laazmi hai to phir Jung hi sahi".

Whenever there is talk of war and jihad, many Hindu brothers and sisters of our country, even some Muslim brothers and sisters, think that war and jihad takes place between Hindus and Muslims, whereas it is not so at all. Infact the teaching of Islam says that those people who are not of your religion and who do not persecute you, do not create obstacles in your religion, but treat you with kindness, then you should also treat them with kindness.Even when Islam said that while eating food, see whether your neighbor is hungry or not? Here too there was no constraint of religion. Infact the money of Zakat can also be given to the people of other religion if they are more needy. Maula Ali Alaihissalam even said that all human beings are brothers; he may be your brother in faith or in humanity.

It is a matter of regret that the Muslims themselves did not spread the teachings of Ahlebait Alaihimussalam, misguided the Muslims as well and showed the wrong picture of Islam to the people of other religions as well. My loved ones! Allah does not belong to any one religion but He belongs to all, but the clerics tried to limit Allah to Muslims.

Then Book of Allah i.e. Quran came not only for Muslims but for all humans and jinn, but the clerics did his job on this too and created distances by making it his property.Our beloved Master, Muhammad Sallallahu Alaihe Wa Aalihi Wa Sallam, was not Rahmatallil Muslimin but Rahmatallil Aalamin i.e mercy for the entire world, but here too Maulvi, by connecting them with one religion, created differences between everyone whereas we should have conveyed the message of Allah to others with love and then it would have been the wish of those people whether they accept our Prophet or reject it, whether they follow the Lord or deny His Oneness, whether they accept or reject the words of their Lord.

I request all my Hindu-Muslim brothers that you should read your history. It was not Hindus who had come to fight with Hussain ibn

Ali Alaihissalam in Karbala, but Muslims and it was not Muslims but Hindus who had come to fight with Pandavas in the war of Mahabharata, and in both the events it is clearly written that there have always been a war of right and wrong Or good and evil.This clearly shows that in every religion there are followers of right and wrong or moral and immoral, we should keep trying to fight the evil forces instead of fighting with each other.

If any sister-daughter is harassed, then the harasser is malicious, oppressive, unrighteous, it should not matter to which religion the sister-daughter who is being harassed belongs to. My loved ones! Supporting the oppressed and rebelling against the oppressor is the message of humanity.

ppp

EIGHTEEN
HUMANITY

Allah Rabb ul Izzat has sent people by making them humans, but they are becoming worse than animals. What is humanity? Why is it important? Ignorant people have become so crazy in their desire to gain this world that they are crushing humanity under their own feet. There is not a single religion which does not teach humanity but nowadays humanity is being killed in the name of religion and people are calling it the victory of religion. Whether it is killing in the name of mob lynching, rioting, terrorism or killings during a war between two countries, they all serve to kill humanity and no religion is behind it.

In every religion there are idiots who consider killing people of other religion in the name of religion as jihad/dharm yudh while they themselves are doing the act of displeasing Allah. The height of barbarity is that now not only between different religions but the people are bend on bloodsheds between the various sects of their own religion. Often such bloodsheds are found between people of the same religion but different sect and if you look at the history of the neighboring country Pakistan, a section of Sunni Muslims bombard the mosques and schools of Shia Muslims and think of themselves as successful Muslims by killing innocent children, when in fact they are the flag bearers of brutality and are partners of the devil.

This becomes even more shameful because Allah has made us 'Ashraful Makhluqat' i.e. the highest and most exalted among all creatures, and therefore our work should have been to help others, to be leaders of humanity, to understand the pain of otehr beings and be considerate to them but we are engaged in killing our own brothers. Even if we put aside this battle of religion and sects, we will find that now even brothers kill each other in the greed of usurping rights in the land.The limit of barbarism is that, now news of parents killing their children or children murdering their parents can also be heard. Think and contemplate what a man was and what has he become?

If we are human, then we should let humanity remain in us. Stop fighting in the name of sect, caste, religion and creed. Repent from wrongdoings, dishonesty, backbiting, sin, evil and fill the whole world with love, brotherhood and humanity. If we feel our religion is right, then we should practice it, rather than imposing it on others. If we want to incline someone towards our religion then we should present our point with a solid reason, and not just by imposing it. Acceptance or Rejection is a matter of understanding and desire of the person in front.

Now let me talk about why there is a bad image of Islam in the hearts of people, especially people of other religions living in India. The first reason is politics, the second reason is the agenda, the third reason is Islamophobia and the fourth reason is low grade media. Politics has also raised the Hindu-Muslim issue for votes in every era, the agenda of Jews and Christians has also been to defame Islam, in which some special forces of almost every religion are trying their level best.Islamophobia has also been spread a lot and the media, which is called the fourth pillar of democracy, losing its dignity and reputation, have done petty actions and deliberately tried to defame Islam. But Allah has made Islam such a flexible religion that it rises as much one tries to defame it. Perhaps this is the reason that despite so many protests and conspiracies, Islam is the fastest growing major religion in the world.

These are those four reasons that are being used by the enemy to damage and discredit the religion, but a wise person is the one who peeks into his own self and then contemplates on his mistakes and deficiencies. Where and how have we gone astray? According to the belief of Muslims, Islam is the religion that came for all humanity and many people say that humanity is the greatest religion, and then Islam is the religion of humanity, but then why aren't we able to convey the true picture of Islam to the people? In actual, the biggest mistake of the Muslims is that they kept killing those who should have been placed like a crown and kept stopping their zikr (praises) and those who were not worthy of praises, they were busy proving them exalted and righteous by calling them Razi-Allah-Razi-Allah.

If you had presented that true image of Muhammad Sallallahu Alaihe wa Alihi wa Sallam in front of the people, in which prays for the one who abuses him, reconciles with the kuffar in Makkah and defends rights, faith and humanity with a sword in his hand when the oppression increases, then hardly anyone would have hated Islam.

If you had presented before the people that image of Maula Ali Alaihis Salaam where he is giving Zakat even in the state of Ruku i.e. helping the poor even during Salat/Namaz, giving Sherbet to his murderer, treating the injured enemies in Jang e Khyber, caring for the orphans of Kufa, hardly anyone would have hated Islam.

If you had presented the character sketch of Fatima Salamullah Alaiha as Islam, how she is standing against the ruler 1400-1500 years ago, fighting for the rights of single women alone, raising her voice against oppression, even being ready to face death for saving Islam, then maybe no one would ever hate Islam.

If you had made Imam Hasan Alaihissalam resemble Islam and presented it to the world that in order to save humanity, to save Deen, to prevent bloodshed, how Imam Hasan Alaihissalam is rejecting the Caliphate or the throne and pardoning his murderer, hardly anyone would have hated Islam, which always stood for humanity.

If you had presented that image of Hazrat Hussain Alaihissalam in front of the people, in which he himself is standing blood-soaked while fighting for deen, humanity, the oppressed, falsehood, and holding the blood-stained innocent Ali Asghar to his chest, and explained that this is Islam, then there would hardly be a person who would dislike Islam.

"Nafrat Islam se nahin
Takhliqi deen se hai Syed,
Tumne pesh hi kiya nahin
Deen e Ahlebayt e Rasool. "

But you called exalted those who usurped the rights of the Prophet's daughter, when Hazrat Ali Alaihissalam went to Kufa, the one who appointed a tyrannical governor in Kufa,you called that caliph a hero, the one who could not handle the Caliphate, he was called the most honourable caliph, the one who snatched the Caliphate from Hazrat Hasan Alaihissalam was called the writer of the scribes or verses of Quran, the one who broke the peace treaty with Hasan Alaihissalam was called RaziAllah, proved adulterers as companions of Prophet,proved the murderers of Hazrat Hussain Alaihissalam righteous, read the odes of those who consider religion to be their rule, moreover you even kept on reading odes of the Mughals who were engrossed in drinking, dancing and singing, you did not even feel ashamed to make that Mughal emperor a Wali (saint), who was the murderer of a true Waliyullah, and then the you complain that why do people misunderstand Islam? You yourself had presented Takhliqi Islam instead of Haqiqi (real) Islam and that's the reason of the poor image of Islam in front of others.

"Jaahil bhi Raziallah, aalim bhi Raziallaah
Naaqis bhi Raziallah, kaamil bhi Raziallah
Ye kaun sa maslak hai, ye kaun sa mazhab hai
Qaatil bhi Raziallah, maqtool bhi Raziallah."

When you yourself forget Hussainiyat and are seen spreading terrorism following Yazidiyat, then will people love you? Were you able to present the real Islam in front of the world through your actions, words, and morals? Definitely not. Moreover, you tried to stop the mentioning of the best personalities of Deen-e-Islam, and today the situation is such that the Muslims, who tell that Islam is the biggest religion of humanity, are not able to prove themselves right and the reason is the leaving of Quran and Ahlebait Alaihimussalam.

My loved ones! Have the fear of Allah and don't stumble at hundreds of doors, return to one door i.e. come to Door of Muhammad and

Aal e Muhammad. Along with Tauheed (Oneness of God), Risalat (Prophethood), hold on to Wilayat and Imamat, move forward holding on to Quran and Ahlebait Alaihimussalam, this is the only way to success. Allahu Akbar Kaseeran Kaseera. Allahumma Salle Ala Muhammad wa Ala Aale Muhammad.

"Insaaniyat na jis mein ho vo aadmi nahi,
Jis mein huzoor qalb na ho bandagi nahi".

ﮊﮊﮊ

NINETEEN

LOVE OF ALL CREATION

My loved ones! We should love all the creatures. For the pleasure of your Lord, you should love every creature created by God. We should show mercy to humans, jinnats, birds, cattle and animals. On the day of Shab e Zarbat, when Maula Ali Alaihissalam left for the mosque, he was surrounded by ducks and then he advised and instructed his family members to take care of these ducks after me, keep giving them grain and water on time and if you cannot take care of them, leave them in a safe place so that they can manage their own sustenance by the command of God.

But Muslims did not behave well neither with any other creatures nor with humans. Of course, humans did not back down from usurping the rights of their brothers and sisters and made such practices common.

Whenever a Muslim talks about love for animals and birds or speaks about showing mercy to them, people of other religions often make fun of him by saying that they themselves eat meat, although if we look at the statistics, we will find that people of almost every religion in India eat chicken, meat, eggs, fish, etc. and our country is also one of the major beef exporting countries.Anyways I won't discuss this because my subject is different.

My loved ones! As we know that there is a food chain in our ecosystem i.e. all the creatures are dependent on each other for food or sustenance. Allah Rabb ul Izzat has created many kinds of creatures, some of which people are unaware of and some they know, there are also many creatures, which people were unaware of before but now they know.

If we think about it, we will find that human beings are also called social animals. There are three types of creatures based on their food, one is Carnivores, the other is Herbivores, and the third is Omnivores. Human beings are Omnivorous, that is, they can eat both meat and vegetarian food.

It should also be noted here that when so many discoveries were not made, we did not have advanced land or advanced seeds, the production of agriculture was also low, then people depended on animals, birds and fish for food in addition to plants and crops. Rather, it will not be incorrect to say that earlier people were more dependent on hunting and the evidence of this is still present and can be found today. There are thousands of years old paintings in Bhima-baithaka etc., which depict humans hunting. If you read about the prehistoric period, it is clearly seen that animals, birds and fish have been used as food.

Another thing worth noting is that animals and birds that are eaten, their population does not decrease, but those that are not eaten are gradually getting extinct or are on the verge of extinction. Then it is also true that we kill hundreds of bacteria in a single breath of ours and it has been proved that there is life in trees and plants, moreover you also know that trees and plants also take their food and some plants even eat insects and such plants are called carnivorous plants like sundews, butterwort, venus flytrap, nepenthes etc., so somewhere or other we are killing all living beings or are forced to do so. Now here it also needs to be mentioned that some beings whose killings can be avoided should be stopped, so in Islam eating the meat of some animals and birds is halal but not obligatory.

A Muslim can be a Muslim without eating meat. Now I answer to those who mock Muslims that eating an animal, bird, etc. as sustenance is one thing, but to cause unnecessary suffering to them is another. Crushing an animal while driving, throwing stones unnecessarily at them or hitting them with sticks unnecessarily or picking them up and throwing them unnecessarily, keeping the animals and birds as pet and not taking care of them properly, not giving them food and drink, etc., all this is another thing.

I do not call something that Allah has made halaal as haraam, but I definitely say that it is not necessary to do that which is not obligatory, and the same is the case with eating meat. I don't think it is right to eat anything solely for taste, yet there is no harm if it is eaten in a small amount according to need. I myself do not like to eat meat, fish etc. and this is my personal practice. However, people should not indulge in the taste of the tongue and eat with moderation.

So my dear people! Stop oppressing the innocent animals, do not kill or persecute them unnecessarily. Whether you are using it in agriculture or for carrying goods, do not overburden the animals and do make them work more than their capacity. We the believers of Ali Alaihissalam love even a horse like Zuljanah and salute his loyalty to the grandson of Rasulullah. My loved ones! Love every creature for the sake of Allah, treat everyone with mercy.Know yourself that you are the noblest of all creatures. Allahu Akbar Kaseeran Kaseera.

"Aye bande tu aadmi se ab, Insan bhi to ban
Yun hi nahi kehlata koi Ashraful Makhlooqat"

ᗰᗰᗰ

TWENTY

RESPONSIBILITIES OF SAADATS

My loved ones! A Saadat's biggest responsibility is to get rid of various sects and gather on one platform and work hard to raise the real religion against the fake religion. To understand the difference between Takhliqi(false)Deen and Haqiqi(real) Deen and to understand how to elevate real deen, you can also read my book, 'Do Islam.....Haqiqi deen aur Takhliqi deen mein fark' and to understand and bridge the gap between Shia-Sunni, you can also read another book of mine 'Shia-Sunni...Ikhtilaf, galatfahmi aur saazish'.

However, I was saying that the Saadats must come forward to promote the real religion against the fake one. I have already written a topic in this book, "Saadat in the society", and in it I have discussed about those responsibilities of a Saadat, through which he can work hard for his home, nation and religion and bring changes in the society. In this topic, I will talk about those responsibilities of a Saadat, which are necessary to connect the entire Ummah with the truth. My loved ones! In our society, there are not only Muslims but there are also people of other religions and creeds, what should be our attitude towards them?, Today, a negative atmosphere against Islam is being created everywhere, how can it be corrected?

First of all, the real Deen must be made to reach all the people, whether they are Muslims or people of other religions, they know and understand Islam that much as they have been told by the clerics and the majority of clerics, delivers speech merely for extortion of money and not for spreading the true religion. Today, people of other religions are considering Islam as bad because the cleric has spread false Islam and the picture of real Islam has not reached the people.We should strive to spread true religion by our actions, character, behavior, manners, habits, nature.

The most important thing for this is to make ourselves the ones who hold the Qur'an and Ahlebait Alaihimusallam and firmly fix on Tawheed, Risalat, Wilayat and Imamat. Then we need to correct our morals and conduct and start treating people with love. Those people of other religions who do not hate us, do not disturb us, do not make bad comments about our religion and God, do not insult our Prophet and Imams , we should dwell with them nicely,infact, we should treat them fairly , that is, their rights need to be fulfilled properly. People of other religions who deliberately target us because of being Muslims, we should try to reconcile with them so that peace and tranquility can be maintained. If one still does not cease their hatred then the last resort is war or jihad, although people should avoid persecuting each other because nothing can be gained by fighting except losses.

"Mazhabi bahas maine ki hi nahin
Faltu aql mujhme thi hi nahin".

One of the biggest mistakes that the Yazidi clerics present in our community have made is that they have considered themselves as the contractors of the religion and have done nothing but harming the religion in the fight for money-grubbing and greed. These clerics are not able to tolerate people from not only other religions but also the people of different sects of their own religion. The terrorists, who attack Shia mosques and schools everyday in the neighbouring country of Pakistan and kill small children, call themselves Sunni Muslims. Will you be able to prove Islam as a religion of peace and unity in this way? The followers of Takhliki (false) Islam had cut off the head of their own Prophet's grandson in Karbala. The Islam which is the symbol of humanity, the Islam which is the religion of peace and tranquility, is the real Islam, against the artificial Islam of the cleric.

The cleric declared, "My Allah, the Allah of the Muslims.", sometimes he announced, "the prophet of the Muslims, my prophet," sometimes he said, "the book of Muslims, our Quran", that is, while heating up the debate of religion he also proved himself to be the contractor of all these whereas this can never be the way of our invitation towards Islam. Who said that all these are for a particular religion or community?, Did you convey the message of truth to other religions?

Today some people of other religions are seen saying abusive things to Allah? What is Allah?, Only the God of Muslims?, No, not at all. Allah means 'The One and Only God' a formless creator whom some call GOD, some Ishwar or Parmatma or Vidhata etc all these are holy and pious names of Allah, whether one calls him in Arabic language or in Hindi language, the only difference is that we believe in one Allah and consider him formless, that is, we do not try to mould him in any form. While some people consider God like a human being or any other creature, which is not correct in our belief because He is the One, He is the Creator and we are the creatures, and that God is not only ours but the Lord of all the worlds, whether anyone believes in Him or not.

Similarly, Kitabullah i.e. Quran is not just a book of Muslims, but it is the word of God sent towards the entire humanity, now whoever wants to, can get guidance by reading it.This is not the book of any particular religion or community, it is the message of God that has come to every human being, whether someone believes it or not, understands it after reading or not, it is his lookout. If you want to convey the message of truth to someone, then convey it with manners, with proofs; never try to impose your beliefs on anyone.

"Sheikh apni rag ko kya karein,
Reshe ko kya karein
Mazhab ke jhagde chhodein
To peshe ko kya karein".

Muhammad Sallallahu Alaihe Wa Aalihi Wa Sallam is not only the prophet of Muslims or Arab people, but he is the prophet and messenger of all the creations of God. Whoever came in his era and who was alive at the time of his announcement of prophethood and after that till the doomsday, every person is his Ummah, whether he belongs to any religion, whether he believes in him or not, whether he loves him or not, it is his deed. So my loved ones! If you want to spread the message of truth to people of other religions, then instead of limiting it to 'mine' start saying 'yours'."Your Lord has sent you a book, your Prophet has said to spread his message" etc.

It is the need of the hour that we, as Muslims, should make our community better, keep helping people, irrespective of religion, if a child is an orphan, then we must keep our hands on his head i.e always support him. Be it a daughter of any religion, if we are present then our presence should give her courage and we should try to keep her dignity safe by being her protector. Irrespective of any religion, we all should come forward to get a poor daughter married. We should treat our neighbours nicely, and try not to hurt them in any way. My loved ones! Remember, we all are brothers, either we are brothers to each other in terms of faith, i.e in relation to Kalma, or we are brothers to each other in terms of humanity. My loved ones! Keep spreading love.

We should always stand with the oppressed, support the poor, the orphan, the widows etc. One should talk about justice and try to spread the message of Karbala and the purpose of Ahlebait Alaihimussalam. Our community will also improve only when we present the conduct, manners and ways of Ahlebayt Alaihimussalam in front of them and even those who have enmity with Islam will love Islam only when they are shown the true picture of the real religion i.e. the picture of the religion of Muhammad and his progeny. Spread the message of Karbala. Allahumma Salle Ala Muhammad wa Ala Aale Muhammad.

"Seekh nafrat ki na de aye 'sada' mazhab koi
Hai usool apna kiye jao mohabbat sabse".

ᗡᗡᗡ

TWENTY-ONE
RULES OF ISLAM

In the same way in which the concept of Islam was changed by Yazidi clerics and they brought Takhliqi Deen against Haqiqi Deen, in the same way they tried to impose their fabricated Shariat(laws)on the people against actual laws and gave illogical fatwas and thus humiliated themselves and defamed Islam too.For example, look at the issue of triple talaq, when in the Qur'an, Allah Rabb ul Izzat himself explained the method of talaq, how to get divoreced by following the Shari'ah within a certain period of time (for more details read Surah Nisa and Surah Talaq.)Then also after the demise of Rasulullah Sallallahu Alayhe Wa Alihi Wa Sallam, some people, following their own will, simultaneously made people obtain triple Talaqs, which was not correct according to the Qur'an, and after that the clerics carried it out and finally became disgraced and discredited the religion as well.

My loved ones! First of all, we have to reach the real Shari'ah and the way is also easy, we have to understand the teachings and instructions of the Qur'an and Ahlebait Alaihimusallam. We have to stick to the Shariat which Muhammad Sallallahu Alaihi Wa Sallam and his progeny has given us and protect ourselves from the fabricated Shariat of the clerics. The fatwas of Yazidi and Marwani clerics which are full of ignorance, hatred, stupidity, and ignorance have also ruined Muslims and harmed the religion. So be it religious issues, worldly issues related to daily life, the solution or fatwas should be taken from a scholar who is a faithful follower of Muhammad Sallallahu Alaihi Wa Alaihi Wassalam and his offsprings.

When we reach the true Deen and Shari'ah, we should try to implement it in our lives. Religion and Shariat are not a burden on anyone, but they are a means to improve your life and gain the pleasure of God while living in this world.For example, we all drink water and it is necessary to drink water in order to live, that is, drinking water is an act that every human being does many times a day, but if we drink this water according to the instructions of Muhammad and his progeny, it is also deen. For example, drink water in a sitting position, drink it in three sips, drink it while facing the Qibla, start with Bismillah and end with Alhamdulillah, do not drink water in the dark, i.e. drink water in the light, etc. Now by drinking water in this way we can please our Lord and along with our health, these practices will be beneficial for us in every way. So my loved ones! When you bring Deen and Shariat into your life, your daily worldly actions also become Deen (religion) and Ibadah(worship).

Fulfilling the commands of Allah, following the instructions of the Qur'an and teachings of Ahlebait Alaihimussalam and following the ways of Muhammad Sallallahu Alaihi Wa Alaihi Wassalam and his progeny in living our lives and doing daily deeds are also part of deen. The meaning is clear that we have to live this worldly life and also have to perform hundreds of everyday tasks, the only difference is that we do every small and big action of our life by our own will, for the sake of people and society or for the sake of Allah.For example, look at marriages, today marriages do not take place simply, in the name of marriage, extravagant spending, dancing, singing, show offs, promiscuity and indecency are becoming common. Then the dowry and the huge procession, puts a heavy burden on the father of a poor daughter, and it becomes even more difficult to arrange for the marriage of orphan girls.So this is the difference, in Deen and it's vice versa.

Nikah is usually for everyone, but the marriage that is done according to the instructions of Muhammad Sallallahu Alaihi Wa Alaihi Wa Aalihi Wassalam is also Deen, is worship, is full of comfort and contains the blessing of Allah. On the contrary, the marriage which contains every wrong doings in the name of marriage serves to please the devil, increases the evils and ultimately harms the Deen and the Ummah. We need to become followers of the Sunnah of our beloved Prophet Muhammad Sallallahu Alaihe Wa Aalihi Wasallam. I have often seen that when a young person tries to follow the Sunnah of Rasool, the people of the society, even his family and parents, try to pull him back instead of encouraging him. For example, if a young man grows a beard, people taunt him that first he should improve his inner self and then outward appearance otherwise it is mere showoff. My loved ones! Disregard these taunts and pay attention to the Sunnah. Of course! Improving your inner self is better than the outer, but it does not mean that the outward appearance should not be improved. If you do it for the sake of others, it will not help you, but if you improve your appearance for the sake of Allah, He will surely purify your inner self.

First, let's talk about the beard. In our society, if a son is born, his parents circumcise him, but when he grows up, they do not encourage him to keep a beard, whereas it is necessary for men to keep a beard, this is Sunnat-e-Muwakkida (confirmed sunnah) and it is wajib in the status, if we see, understand and consider that every Prophet and Messenger from Adam Alaihissalam to

Muhammad Sallallahu Alaihe Wa Alaihi Wa Sallam has kept a beard and encouraged to keep it. At the same time, it was also ordered that if one wants to avoid following other religions, especially the Jews and Christians, and if one wants to try to follow Rasoolullah, then keeping a beard is considered as an obligation. But in our society men left the external Sunnah that would be taken with them to the grave, then how will he implement on the Sunnahs that improve the inner being, it is a matter of great contemplation.

So my loved ones! We should continue to follow Haqiqi Deen, Haqiqi Shariat, Sunnah of Rasool, teachings of Ahlebait of Rasool and bring down Deen and Shariat in our lives in such a way that they become a part of our lives. Every moment of our life, every second, should be spent in obedience of God, obedience of the Messenger and obedience of the Prophet. Let us hold on to the Qur'an and the Ahl al-Bayt and continue to advance in the path of spiritual knowledge and become so passionate and engrossed in the love of Allah, and destroy ourselves that our Allah gets pleased with us. Allahu Akbar Kaseeran Kaseera. Allahumma Salle Ala Muhammad Wa Ala Aale Muhammad.

"Shariyat se hi banta hai,
   kanoon e zindagi magar,
   Mulla ki shariyat aur hai,
   Allah ki shariyat aur."

ᗡᗡᗡ

TWENTY-TWO
CONSPIRACY OF THE UMMAH

My loved ones, saadat and lovers of Ahlebait! The ummah had started plotting openly against the Ahlebait Alaihimussalam just after the demise of Prophet Muhammad Sallallahu Alaihi Wa Aalihi Wassalam, which I will describe in the upcoming sections. In this topic, I am talking about the conspiracies of the Ummah which are going on in the current period and are working to mislead people from the right path. First of all, we will talk about the conspiracies of the various sects of the Ummah and then later we will talk about the conspiracies of those Muslims who call themselves Muslims.

Yes my dear ones! It is a bitter truth that the people who called themselves Muslims have not only caused trouble to the progeny of Allah's Messenger but have also killed them, and the killing is not just that they assassinated them but also cut their body into pieces. They desolated the house of Rasulullah. May the curse of Allah be upon the oppressors and enemies of Ahlebayt Alaihimusallam.

From the beginning, some Jews and Christians have tried to defame Islam and now people of other religions are also actively participating in it. Similarly, there are many organizations who are working hard day and night to bring a new world order and in fact their hard work is for 'Dajjal', they are engaged in proving Satan as God and Dajjal as God and are working against Imam Mehdi Alaihissalam. The sad thing is that the Muslims have ceased to support their Imam and the enemies of Islam have continued their hard work day and night. This system has gradually spread all over the world and is filling people's subconscious minds with their teachings and beliefs in such a way that now people themselves cannot understand when they went astray and reached the void. The widespread of Prostitution, promiscuity, adultery etc. are a deliberate conspiracy of these systems and they have succeeded in their tricks because most of the Muslims have become heedless.

Most of the mosques and pulpits are occupied by Yazidis and today they are not able to bark at Ahlebait as openly as they used to, but still slowly and gradually they are continuously dissolving poison in the hearts of the people. For example, comparing Sahaba Raziallah Anhuma with Ahlulbayt Alaihimusallam, singing praises of sahabas instead of Ahlebayt Alaihimusallam and that too mentioning only 6-7 Sahaba in the name of Zikr e Sahaba and forgetting the rest of Sahabas, spreading Takhliqi (made up) deen instead of Haqiqi (true) deen. Maula Ali Alaihissalam's enemies are hypocrites who spoil people's faith by pretending to be pious.

There are many sects in the world who bark against Ahlebait Alaihimusallam, but the worst sect among all those has been the one, one of whose maulvi barked at the daughter of Rasoolullah, Fatimah Salaamullah Alaiha and started accusing her of falsehood on the issue of Fadak, while Fatimah Salamullah Alaiha is the most truthful and the most righteous. May the curse of Allah be on such a worst cleric. Now, whichever sect that Maulvi is associated with, you need to find yourself and contemplate on it and avoid such worst sects that spread fitnah and return to Deen e Haqiqi Islam (The true Religion).

There is an organization in India which some Muslims have designed in order to get scholarship, reservation etc. by proving themselves backward. As a Saadat, we all remained silent because we had no problem if any worldly deprived gets help through reservation, but they could not get any reservation, as a result they reached the peak of madness and started accusing Saadats of having superiority complex and suppressing the Pasmanda community. Although the truth has been the opposite, the believers have honoured Saadat as the progeny of the Messenger of God, but the numbers of those who praise him have been few and the number of those who abuse them has always been greater. The most oppressed and persecuted family in the Ummah of Prophet Muhammad has been that of his own progeny, however, Saadats never demanded any sort of reservation, nor sought sympathy from the people by proving themselves oppressed.

It is also a fact that whenever any section of the Ummah got the chance, they persecuted and even killed the members of Ahlebait, but the reservation-hungry Muslims, in order to prove themselves oppressed, made false, dirty, filthy accusations against Maula Ali, Hasnain Karimain and their offsprings. It is also a matter of wonder that Saadats, who were chopped and beheaded, and their bodies were crushed and trampled by horses, are called oppressors and the real oppressors of Saadats, those beasts who even killed the six-month-old innocent Ali Asghar are pretending to be oppressed today.

There is no concept of caste in Islam, and clan, family, and lineage are merely for identifying each other. The numbers of those who love Saadats have been very few in every era and they respect Saadats because of their blood relations with Rasulullah. It is not the case that Saadat has been called superior and the rest of the Muslims are inferior.Saadats have never mentioned caste discrimination in any of their books, although it is a matter of irony that the majority of those who call themselves backward, consider that Khan Sahib as superior and support him who has deliberately made a false and absurd attempt to forcefully add such a concept of casteism in Islam.

"Firqa- bandi hai kahin aur kahin zaatein hain ,
Kya zamaane mein panapne ki yahi baatein hain."

Before the emergence of Imam Mahdi, this ummah will once again be seen bent on mass killing of Saadats and I think this oppression will be done in the name of honour of Sahabas and the group which claims to be so called Muslims will call Sadaats impudent of the Companions of the Prophet and kill and loot them. However, this is also a big fitnah that has arisen in the present era where major Sahabas like Hazrat Salman Farsi, Hazrat Abuzar Ghaffari, Hazrat Miqdad Ibn Amr (Miqdad Al Aswad), Malik Bin Harith (Malik Al-Ashtar), Hazrat Hujr Bin Adi, Hazrat Bilal Bin Rabah, Habib Ibn A Muzahir Al-Asadi are not even mentioned and instead of thousands and millions of other Sahabas, only six or seven Companions of their choice are imposed on others. An amazing thing is that only those Sahabas are highlighted, for whom controversial events are found, about whom it is also written that they persecuted the Ahlebait.

For example, Abul Yazid Muawiya is proved to be superiorand Raziyallah, that Abul Yazid who fought a war against Maula Ali Alaihissalam, during whose caliphate Ali Alaihissalam was abused from the pulpit, who broke the peace treaty with Hasan Alaihissalam and broke the covenant, who usurped the rights of Hazrat Hussain Alaihissalam and imposed a tyrant and inferior caliph like Yazid on the head of the Ummah. Now, instead of Hazrat Salman, Abul Yazeed is being called the standard of Sahabiyyah and whoever does not consider Yazid's father as Sahaba is being proved as a disbeliever.

So my loved ones! Understand the conspiracies of the ummah and start spreadingthe truth, it is already too late, if it is delayed more then it will be almost impossible to bring the necessary reforms and changes. The time is near when the Imam will reappear, spread deen e Haq, and keep trying to thwart the conspiracies of the devils. May Allah help us all. Allahu Akbar Kaseeran Kaseera.

"Kuch baat hai ki hasti,
Mit ti nahin hamari,
Sadiyon raha hai dushman,
Daur-e-jahaan hamaara".

❧❧❧

TWENTY-THREE
ALIYUN WALIULLAH

The clerics of the Ummah are busy instigating fights between people in the greed of bribery. They are engaged in obeying, persuading and imposing the beliefs of their own sect. At the same time, some intelligent people talk about unity, but the problem is that if it is to be done, then how? When we believe in the same one God, one Quran, one Prophet and have similar beliefs and faiths then why are we divided into so many sects? Why is sectarianism becoming so common?

People often say that we should unite on the basis of the Quran, unite on the basis of the kalma, etc., etc., but unity cannot be brought because the foundations on which we call for unity, those very foundations are already baseless. The truth is that this ummah can never be united because the ummah which did not unite on the call of Imam Hussain Alaihissalam, how can it be united on our call. However, we still try to bring unity so that any "Hurr" can come out of the various camps towards truth.

So my loved ones, there is only one way to attain unity, that is the issue that has spread anxiety should be rectified and then we should be united on the basis of which we are divided, and it is clear that those issues are not Tawheed, Risalat, Quran or Kalma because every sect has same beliefs on these. My loved ones! Wilayat-e-Ali Alaihissalam is the one issue, that is, people did not believe in Wilayat-e-Ali, and those who did, did not believe in the way they should have believed, and this is the only reason why the ummah has been divided. They are divided into Jamaat and Maslaks.

If we want the ummah to be united, then first of all we have to hold on to Aliyun Waliullah, Qur'an and Ahlebayt Alaihimusallam. Aliyun Waliullah is not just a slogan but it is that belief of ours which makes us true Momineen and separates us from the Nasbi and the Kharjis. Aliyun Waliullah is that announcement that is still enough to make the enemy sleepless. All Saadats and followers of Ahlebait Alaihissalam should spread this slogan and keep conveying the true religion to the people.

What is the threat that the kalma reciting Yazidi clerics have from Aliyun Waliullah? The answer is that if Aliyun Waliullah is accepted then the true religion of Allah will spread and the Takhliqi (fake) religion of the Mullah will vanish. Aliyun Waliullah is bounty, and the clerics religion comprises of petty funding.Aliyun Waliullah has humanity while Mullah's deen is terror, Aliyun Waliullah preaches Haq (truth)while Mullah's Deen preaches Haq-Talfi, (violation of truth).Aliyun Waliullah spreads truth while Mullah's Deen spreads Yazidiyat.

After the demise of Rasulullah Sallallahu Alaihe wa Aalihi Wasallam, when his daughter was deprived of her rights on Fadak, by the then formed government, she became the first lawyer woman and fought with the caliph of the time and defeated the ummah who wanted to convert the caliphate into a government and the true religion and thus saved Aliyun Waliullah as well as the true deen. Of course, she could not get her Fadak back, but she definitely showed the difference between right and wrong by rebelling.When Hazrat Ali Alaihissalam also got worldly caliphate, then he tried to correct the damage done in the religion after the demise of Rasulullah and he was successful to a great extent, but seeing the destruction of Takhliqi (fake) Deen, people martyred Maula Ali Alaihissalam himself.

Even after this, the process of spreading Haqiqi Deen and Aliyun Waliullah did not stop the Ahlebait of Rasulullah and their followers and slaves continued to sacrifice their lives in every era but continued to uphold the right and In Sha Allah, after the emergence of Imam Mahdi. , the true Deen will prevail and the call of Aliyun Waliullah will be echoed all around. My loved ones! If you want unity and betterment, then spread Aliyun Waliullah, conveys the message of Ghadeer e Khum to the people, hold fast on to the Quran and Ahlebait Alaihimusallam, this is the only way to get salvation and achieve success. Allahu Akbar Kaseeran Kaseera.

"Zahra se pucho kya hai, Aliyun Waliullah
Iske liye Batool ka do baar ghar jala,
Baghdaad, Shaam o Kufa Khurasan o Karbala,
Ummat ne Fatima ko kahan dukh nahin diya."
    "Sab kuchh lutaaya deen ki hifazat ke waaste,
Zahra ujad gayi hai wilayat ke waaste,
Darbaar mein bachaane gayi Fatima Zahra
Aliyun Waliullah, Aliyun Waliullah, Aliyun Waliullah...."

ﭒﭒﭒ

TWENTY-FOUR

REBELLING AGAINST HAQ DEEN

Rebelling against Haq Deen (The True Religion)

In the presence of Rasoolullah, his Ummat did not stop following the deen, rather were bent on proving their piousness but after the demise of Rasulullah, this Ummah got divided into five parts. One is the family of Muhammad i.e his progeny (Ahlebait e Rasool). The second were the Sahabas who were faithful towards Prophet and his progeny. Thirdly, those who turned away from Deen and became apostates and again involved into Kufr and Shirk. Fourthly, those who called themselves Muslims but tried to change Islam from religion to governance and came against Ahlulbayt, and fifthly those who chose to remain silent due to fear/greed or some other reasons, i.e. neither supported Ahlebait Alaihimussalam nor showed support to the then existing government. Later, all the new beliefs and Takhliqi (fake) Deen that emerged among the Muslims came out of the third, fourth and fifth divisions.

There were some people in the era of Prophet too who considered Prophethood and religion as means of gaining power, but they also knew very well that it was not possible to establish the power of oppression by fighting Muhammad Sallallahu Alaihe wa Aalihi Wasallam and his then some of them considered their personal gain and by accepting Islam, as Muslims began to claim faith, but in reality they always remained a hypocrites. There have been some Muslims who persecuted Rasulullah Sallallahu Alaihi wa Aalihi wa Sallam throughout their lives and fought with Muhammad Rasulullah till the last breath, but when the conquest of Makkah took place and there was no way to escape, they came rubbing their noses and read the kalma with a heavy heart.Although the intention with which they had recited the kalma became apparent only after the demise of the Prophet, their hatred grew so much that their fierce face was seen in Karbala. When the so called Muslims who called themselves the Ummah of Muhammad Rasoolullah became thirsty for the blood of the offsprings of Ali to such an extent that they even killed and martyred the six-month-old innocent Ali Asghar.

There were two issues in the heart of the majority of the Ummah, one was the greed to rule and the other was hatred for Ali Alaihissalam. The greed of governing can be understood and if one does not understand the beauty of Islam, then he will not obviously understand the difference between the Islamic caliphate and the worldly government but why they hated ALI ALAIHISSALAM and I would like to elaborate a little on this. The fact is that when stones were pelted on Rasulullah Sallallahu Alayhi Wasallam, a ten or twelve year old child was trying to protect Rasulullah from the infidels. At the occasion of 'Daawat e Zulasheera' when no one supported the Prophet, it was the same innocent child who raised his hands repeatedly to extend his support and finally Rasulullah accepted the promise of his helper, that child was no one other than my Maula Ali Alaihissalam.

After that, whether it was Badr or Hunain, Ohad, Khandaq or Khyber or any other battle, everywhere only Ali was seen. In Jang-e-Ohad, when the Kuffaar (enemies) thought that they would kill Rasulullah, suddenly Ali Alaihissalam came there and rescued Rasulullah from there, when even the Sahaaba Raziullah had also fled, leaving Rasulullah alone in the field. Although later they repented and there is a clear mention of this incident in Surah Tauba of the Quran. After that be it the battle of Khandaq, Khyber or victory of Mecca, Ali Alaihissalam was made the leader and flag bearer of the Prophet. Even the hypocrites along with the enemies were troubled by this and they began keeping enmity and jealousy against Ali Alaihissalam.

When Rasulullah was returning from his last Hajj, he ordered everyone to stop at Ghadir e Khumm , made a pulpit there, gave a sermon and finally made Ali alaihissalam his heir and successor or we can say announced him as his inheritor. In fact Ali Alaihissalam was also declared as the 'Maula' of everyone, all the Nasbi, Kharji and hypocrite people were burnt to ashes, but then they could not do anything. Despite of Rasulullah's commands, just after his demise the people began to attack and oppress Ahlebait Alaihimusallam and began to build and expand their rule. Amma Fatimah SalamullahAlaiha was deprived of her property i.e the land of Fadak, the rights were taken away from Ali, and the Ummah rejected the Caliphate created by Allah, and chose their own Caliphate with their allegiance.

"Ummat ne hi maana nahi, Apne Nabi ke hukm ko
Musalmaano ne thukra diya, Khud rab ke hi kaanoon ko".

Who is superior between Ahlebait and Sahaba?, Who is right among Shia and Sunni?, Get out of such battles like we are right and you are wrong and search for the truth. The fight is not between two people but between verse and Tradition, between history and Hadith because in every era after the demise of Rasulullah till now, a lot of efforts were made to replace Haqiqi Deen with Takhliqi Deen. Distortions have been brought in Shariat, instead of the orders of Allah and Rasoolullah, their own religion was enforced and imposed on the people. Infact, the real religion has been suppressed to such an extent that now people consider only the made up religion as Islam, and if you present the real Islam to them, they feel as if a new religion is being told.

"Takhliqi deen ko hi samajhte hain haqiqi,
Ummat ko gumrahi se bhala kaise nikaloon?"

If we contemplate, we will find that it is not that people did not only accept Ali Alaihissalam as their leader, but Muslims even rejected the orders of Allah, Rasoolullah, Quran, and also rejected Ahlebait Alaihimussalam. The height is that even after this they did not get peace, and they went on killing Ali Alaihissalam and his children and this process continued for generations. Not one or two but thousands of perverts have arisen due to this practice of devilishness, rebellion of religion but I am talking about one pervert as an example, rest you can guess yourself. Our clerics stresses on Namaz the most, so lets understands this. Today there are four Imams in Sunnis and none of them are from the progeny of Rasulullah, they perform Namaz in four different ways, namely Hanafi, , Shafai, Maliki and Hambali. Their followers consider their respective Imams as correct and others as wrong. Those who are more sensible say that all the four Imams are correct; you can follow any one of them. Follow the ways of anyone of them as per your choice.

Now the matter of concern is that how our beloved Rasoolullah Sallallahu Alaihe wa Alaihi wa Sallam used to perform Namaz?, Did he performed Namaz in four different ways?, If yes! So why should we pray in the any one way? and If not! Then, how did Rasulullah perform Salah or Namaz?, Out of four, which Sunni Imam's method of Namaz is correct and which three are wrong?

Some people say that God sees your intention while praying instead of the way one prays, where hands are being kept during prayer etc. Then why are there hundreds of rules in the name of Farz, Wajib, Sunnah, etc and if these are important then why does it not matter what is the right way?

The truth is that this difference in the way of prayer is also the result of rebelling against the true religion and creating a fake religion. They kept killing those from whom the ummah should have learned, and those who used to run away while Rasulullah was praying to watch games, spectacles, and bazaars, even during Friday prayers, kept asking them the way to pray. Think about it, today if a person goes out after praying only two rakats on Friday, then the congregation looks at him with contempt as if he has not performed the full prayer while he has already performed the obligatory prayer and these so called Sahabas used to get up and leave in the middle of the obligatory Friday prayer, even when Rasulullah Sallallahu Alaihi wa Sallam would be doing the Imamat himself, how many details would they (Sahaba) know about the prayer?

But alas, the ummah asked those who were not in prayer and killed those who had every little knowledge of prayer and I am not claiming this personally that some Sahabas used to run away during the daily and Friday prayers too (While as per our faith, not every person is a Sahaba who found the age of a Prophet, believed and met Rasulullah, but the Sahaba were even better than the Kalma reciters of that period. We do not consider people like the father of Yazid as Sahaba, but it is not that we dislike the Sahabas rather we are ready to sacrifice our lives for the Sahabas like Hazrat Salman Farsi Raziullah and Inshallah we will continue to do so in the future). You can understand the rest yourself by reading Surah Juma.

"Quran o Ahlebait se munh apne modkar,
Gumraah ho gaye hain sab Ali ko chhodkar".

Here I have given only one example, and that too of that action, which is recommended the most by our clerics. Now you can think yourself, if you pay attention to each and every action, then in the same way you will understand the difference between the real religion and the artificial, made up one and the reality will automatically dawn upon you. My loved ones! Hold on to Quran and Ahlebait Alaihimussalam and return to Deen-e-Haqiqi i.e. Haqiqi Islam (real Islam) as this is the only way to success.

Allahu Akbar Kaseeran Kaseera. Allahumma Salle Ala Muhammad wa Ala Aale Muhammad.

ﻉﻉﻉ

TWENTY-FIVE
WHO IS A KAFIR?

Muslim clerics have spread a word that all those who read Kalma are Muslims whereas the word Muslim or Musalmaan is used for the followers of Islam and all those who do not read Kalma are Kafirs. But the truth is different from this. The word Kafir has three meanings -

1. The one who does not accept the right/ truth, the one who denies it.
2. Concealing the truth even after knowing it.
3. One who lives against the truth, one who goes against the law.

Now, if decisions are made based on this definition, then why should people of other religions be called infidels or Kaafirs? Whereas Muslims themselves will not be able to prove their faith and Islam. Those whom the Maulvi calls kafir, no matter whoever they are, at least they are not the killers of the family of Rasulullah Sallallahu Alayhi Wa Alihi WaSallam, his progeny and offsprings,while those whom the Maulvi Hazrat are trying to prove 'Raziallah' are the ones who have either persecuted Ahlebait Alaihimusallam or assassinated them.

The beliefs of the clerics are also very strange, in the beliefs of these ignorant people, Hazrat Abu Talib who raised Muhammad Sallallahu Alayhi wa Alihi Wasallam in his lap, protected and supported him, he is a disbeliever and the ancestors of Yazid who constantly troubled Rasulullah Sallallahu Alayhi Wa Alihi Wasallam and his progeny are so called 'Raziallah'.

Maula Ali Alaihissalam whom Rasulullah Sallallahu Alaihe Wa Aalihi Wasallam called Kul e Iman (The completion of faith) the clerics issued fatwas of Kufr (infidelity) on him. If we look at the Islamic history, we will find that after the demise of Rasulullah to this day, 'Aal e Rasool' and 'Ghulam-e-Ahlebait-e-Rasool' are persecuted in various ways.

Those Saadats who are heedless and have left their forefathers and are trapped in the clutches of the clerics, they may be saved from these fatwas, but it is not possible that a Saadat who spreads the truth and 'Haqiqi Deen' and is not called Rafzi, Kafir, Gustakh e Sahaba etc. According to my knowledge, the ummah has placed the most accusations and fatwas on the Syeds, rest Allah knows best.

I do not know why but the clerics possess a strange anxiety to prove themselves right and others wrong. It is not that they call only the adherents of other religions infidels, but they also call the people of their own religion, who read the kalma as infidels. For them, a Muslim is one who obeys their Yazidi-Marwani peers. Those who promote sectarianism, bribery, ignorance, hatred of Ahlebait, terrorism etc.

Those who give their lives for the salvation and protection of the true religion, those who believe in Ahlebayt Alaihimusallam, are infidels or kaafirs according to them while in reality, there is hardly anyone more than these Marwani-Yazidi clerics who are bent on infidelity as much as these Yazidi clerics themselves.

By the command of Allah, the Prophet of Allah, Muhammad Sallallaahu Alaihi wa Aalihi Wa-sallam, announced the Maulaiyat of Ali Alaihissalam himself, with his blessed tongue, but the people did not accept the truth and denied it. The truth was deliberately hidden, suppressed, and infact false hadiths were also fabricated in order to put down 'Fazilat e Ahlebait'.

Finally a large congregation of Muslims went astray and unfortunately the people stooped so low to the extent of enraging a war against Haqq (Truth). In this way, a large group of Muslims themselves committed kufr and are carrying the burden of it till today, but instead of admitting their sin, being ashamed, instead of repenting, they are distributing certificates of kufr to the followers of other sects and religions. Maulvi Sahib! First, get yourself out of the blasphemy of Yazidiyyah and Marwaniyyah, then continue issuing fatwas on others. Allahu Akbar Kasiran Kasir. Allahu Rabi, Allahu Rahman, Allahu Kareem, Allahu Rahim.

I live in India, so I am presenting an example from here. Today there are many Hindu brothers and sisters who support Panjatan Pak and there are many Muslims who not only believe Yazid and his father and grandfather but also impose them on everyone. Just imagine if many Maulai Muslims and Hindu brothers and sisters are forgiven on the basis of their belief in Tawheed i.e. a formless monotheism and the love of Ahlebait Alaihimusallam and the ones who call themselves promoters of Islam and call others kafir-kafir,such

Yazidi Mullahs are thrown into hell on the basis of their hatred towards Ahlebait. Then what will be the condition of these Yazidi Mullahs on the day of Resurrection?

"Kaafir jo keh rahe ho har ek haq-parast ko,
Khul jaye asliyat to tum badnaam rahoge,
Tum hi iblees ke dajjaal ke ek pairokaar ho,
Roz e hashr bhi yazidi tumhi naakaam rahoge".

ﻉﻉﻉ

TWENTY-SIX

REJECTION OF GOD'S COMMAND

Most of the people who call themselves and are called Muslims have rejected the commands of God and disobeyed the decisions of God, and further took wrong decisions from their own minds and tried to impose those decisions on the people. Not only in the matter of Ahlebait e Rasool, but also in matters related to religion and world, they tried to enforce their own rules. For example, giving instant triple talaq, 'Hajj Tamatto' that is, performing Hajj and Umrah together, preventing women from going to mosques and not making room for them in mosques etc.

Although Maula Ali Alaihissalam opposed all these fitnahs and when he got the caliphate, he also worked to remove all these evil changes brought to the society and the Shariah. Muslims had to accept his commands but some rectifications are not accepted till today, although the Shias have accepted it to a large extent.

The first Caliph/Imam/'Wasi e Rasool' appointed by Allah in this Ummat-e-Muhammad was rejected by the Ummah itself and they chose their own Caliph. However, the thing of laughter and regret is that the people who chose the first caliph themselves are waiting for the last caliph and Imam and they believe that the last Imam will appear and we will pledge allegiance to him. When the last imam will appear and you pledge allegiance to him, then why weren't you able to recognize the first Imam?, Why can't you pledge allegiance to him? And if a mistake was then committed why couldn't you rectify it till now? Anyways here too the ambivalence of the Yazidi clerics and his advocates is clearly visible.

The real religion that Allah Ta'ala sent to the world, people tried to destroy it themselves and imposed their own Takhliqi (fake) religion on people. Yazidi Maulvi Sahab also changed the authentic Shariat that Allah Rabb ul Izzat had sent down to us and imposed his own Takhliqi Shariat on the people.

The teachings of the Prophet of Allah were rejected and the two important things that the Prophet of Allah had given were rejected. And instead of paying compensation of Prophethood ('Ajr e Risalat') this Ummah killed the progeny of Rasulullah. The matter of rejecting the commands of God did not end here, infact the height was that the 'Ulil-Amr', i.e. Aaimma-e-Ahlebait Alaihimusallam, given by Allah, was rejected. Still, when they did not get peace, the Muslims assassinated the Imams in every period. What a pity! They killed those from whom they should have learned knowledge, and those who should have been punished were placed on high pedestals and thrones.

The attitude of the majority of Muslims towards Allah's creation is condemnable.The practice of usurping rights of one's relatives-neighbors and even one's own brothers and sisters are common. Which Islam is this? Which religion is this? Indeed, this is the result of holding on to others, instead of the Quran and Ahlebait

Alaihimusallam. The creatures, whom Allah had sent by making the most superior one(Ashraful Makhlooqat) that same creature today remains the worst because of their actions and turning away from the commandments of their Lord.

"Hashr ke roz hoga saamna,
Maalik e yaumiddeen se,
Husn e amal bhi saath rakh, Rab ko manaana hai,
Chhodkar Rab ke hukmon ko, Payambar se rakhi doori,
Wahaan apne Nabi ko bhi to Tujhko munh dikhaana hai."

Just think and contemplate, Allah made you the superior of all creatures, then blessed you with the wealth of faith, blessed you with the wealth of Islam, sent you in the community of your Habib, Imam-e-ambiya i.e. the leader of the prophets, in that community whose Ummah is the leader of all Ummahs, that is, we should have become superior in our actions, character, virtues and humanity and in every respect.

Not only humans, be it jinn or animals or birds, even insects, we should have been useful for each and every creation of God, should have shown mercy to all, but alas, our Muslim brothers and sisters, by following the Takhliki Deen of clerics, became the worst people of the best Ummah of the best Prophet.

I repeat one thing again and again that, "My loved ones! Hold on to the Quran and Ahlebait Alaihimussalam, as this is the only path that leads to Allah and the success of both worlds. Every mischief, evil, fitna has spread just because we have left Quran and Ahle-bait Alaihimussalam and everything will be fine only when we return to Quran and Ahle-bait Alaihimussalam without stumbling here and there, from door to door." May Allah Rab-ul-Izzat make us all more doers than hearers and give us the ability to follow the true religion and spread it among the masses.

"Hussainiyat ko chhodkar,
  Takhliqi deen par chale.
Hukm e khuda bhula diya,
  Khud hi Musalmaan ne."

❧❧❧

TWENTY-SEVEN

HAQQ E MUHAMMAD

No one can do what Muhammad Sallallahu Alaihe wa Aalihi Wasallam has done for this Ummah. The wives of the Prophet are more than a mother to the believers of the Ummah, hence they are called Ummul Momineen. And He Rasulullah Sallallahu Alaihe wa Aalihi Wasallam is the Messenger of Allah for the Ummah, and whatever he has done for the Ummah, even a father cannot do that much for his children. The ummah cannot repay the favor of its Prophet even if he wants to, since he has conveyed the word of God (Kitabullah) to us, his slaves.

However, the first right of Rasulullah over the ummah was that the ummah should have paid Azr-e-Risalat and in Azr-e-Risalat, wealth was not asked for, but only the love and support of His progeny was rather sought and this was not said by Rasulullah Sallallahu Alayhi wa Aalihi Wasallam himself but by the command of Allah, that too when the verse in the Quran was revealed that, "I do not ask you for any reward for the Messengership/Prophethood but only that you love and help my offsprings i.e. Ahlebait.", but the Ummah could not give this compensation instead they killed Panjatan, the Imams, the Ahlebait, and others by poisoning them, tormenting them, cutting them to death, and martyred all of Muhammad's progeny. Those who survived were persecuted and continue to be so to this day.

I would also like to give a little explanation of the word "Mawaddat". In the Quran, the word 'hubb' has appeared for love, that is, where love is spoken about, it has been written as love, but the clerics have translated it 'Mawaddat' as love (Mohabbat) or Habb/Hubb/Hibb, although both are different words. I am giving an example to explain the difference between 'Mohabbat' and 'Mawaddat' - a turtle or a crocodile loves water, that is, they like to live in water, but it is not necessary for them to live in water, and they can live without being in water. But a fish has 'Mawaddat' for water that is it dies when taken out of water.

In the same way a believer does not only love Ahlul Bait but also has 'Mawaddat' for them, i.e. he cannot live without Ahlebait Alaihimusallam. We can also call 'Muwaddat' as selfless love. The ummah should have obeyed the orders of their God and the Prophet and kept 'Mawaddat' with Ahlebayt Alaihimusallam, but the Ummah presented the corpses and blood of his family to their Prophet in the name of Azr-e-Risalat. Allahu Akbar.

Whatever message Rasulullah Sallallahu Alaihe Wa Aalihi Wasallam conveyed to the Ummah, the teachings and training, the Sunnah, the religion and Shariah, the way of living life, morality, manners and knowledge should have followed properly by the Ummah, but the ummah left the Quran and Ahl al-Bayt Alaihimusallam first just after the demise of Rasool, in contradiction to what Rasulullah Sallallahu Alaihe Wa Aalihi Wasallam had ordered, that is to hold on to the Quran and Ahl al-Bayt to avoid going astray.After that, the ummah replaced Haqiqi Deen with Takhliqi Deen and replaced Haqiqi Shariat with Takhliqi

Shariat.

Far from trying to honour their Messenger, the Ummah even rejected the commands of their Prophet. Yazidi clerics used the Prophet's name to promote extortion and spread sectarianism. On one hand, they declared themselves as Aashiq-e-Rasool (Lovers of the Prophet) and were also engaged in opposing Ahlebait-e-Rasool on the other.

"Rasool e paak se ulfat aur Unki aal se nafrat,
Hamein in sarfiron ka ye aqeeda, achha nahin lagta".

The Ummah did not spread the teachings of Muhammad or Aal e Muhammad, but the main problem was that they themselves did not possess such status that people would listen to these Marwani clerics. An evil way was thus paved and in it those hadiths of Rasulullah Sallallahu Alaihi wa Alihi Wasallam which used to demolish their satanic beliefs were removed.

The hadiths which glorified Ahlebait Alaihmussalam were removed and people started writing and spreading false hadiths attributing to Rasoolullah in order to mislead people by bringing Rasoolullah's name in the interface and to use fabricated hadiths as a shield for their false beliefs. At the same time, describing the glory of their own ancestors, they also started fabricating false hadiths so that they could make them stand against the Ahlebait. The need of the hour is to bring the reality of Yazidi clerics openly in front of the people so that people can return to the truth.

Today, all the Saadats and Ghulamaan e Ahlebait should unite and support the right and openly fight against the wrong. Spread Haqiqi Deen, Haqiqi Shariat, Zikr-e-Ahlebait Alaihimussalam and Zikr-e-Karbala. Get knowledge, investigate. Improve yourself, your family members and keep trying to improve your surroundings and society continuously. Allahu Akbar Kaseeran Kaseera. Allahumma Salle Ala Muhammad wa Ala Aale Muhammad.

"Kisi ghamgusaar ki mehnaton ka ye khoob maine sila diya,
Jise mere gham ne ghula diya, use maine dil se bhula diya".

ﮓﮓﮓ

TWENTY-EIGHT
HAQQ E FATIMA

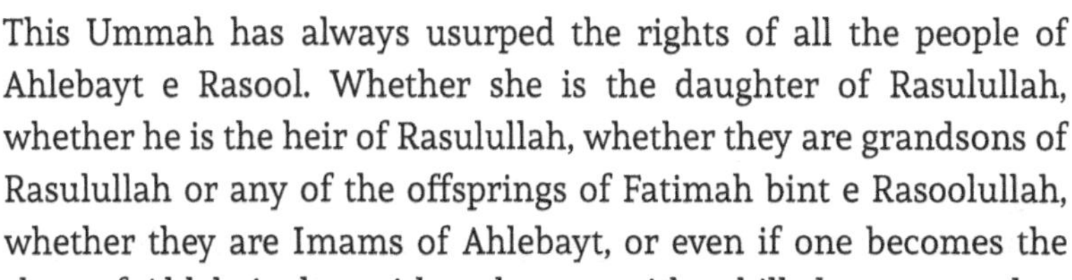

This Ummah has always usurped the rights of all the people of Ahlebayt e Rasool. Whether she is the daughter of Rasulullah, whether he is the heir of Rasulullah, whether they are grandsons of Rasulullah or any of the offsprings of Fatimah bint e Rasoolullah, whether they are Imams of Ahlebayt, or even if one becomes the slave of Ahlebait then either they are either killed or tortured to such an extent that a common man would succumb. But in the Ahlebait of Rasulullah, I believe the right of Fatima Salamullah Alaiha is the greatest of all and I have my own arguments behind it.

The first argument is that, Fatima Salamullah Alaiha is the daughter of Rasoolullah and because of this relationship she has been close to Rasulullah, more than anyone else .She is the only child and can be called a part of Rasulullah.

The second argument is that after the demise of Rasulullah, she was the first whose rights were usurped and her Fadaq was taken away, which was one of the biggest mistakes of this Ummah. If this had not happened, maybe today the scenario would have been different, however, whatever happens, happens only with the will of God and Allah is the best knower, the one who is just.

The third argument is that the distance between Shia and Sunni is because of hundreds of differences, but there are also some major reasons that hinder unity and one of those major reasons is the issue of Fadak. Although most of the Saadats, or let me say that those Saadats who have formed their faith from Door of Ahlebait and not by listening to the clerics and in whose family there is no heedlessness but the training of the children is done under the shadow of the Quran and the Ahlebait, all those Saadats firmly believe that Fadak was the true right of Fatima Salamullah Alaiha.

I am not saying at all that you should unnecessarily accuse any historical figure, nor am I saying that you should not believe anyone, your belief is your own. I just say that when it comes to truth, the truth should be stated openly, and the truth is that Fadak belonged only to Fatima Salamullah Alaiha, it should not have been taken away from her, and when it was taken away, and Fatima Salamullah Alaiha demanded it, it should have been duly returned to her immediately. Even then if it was not given, then when the daughter of Rasulullah went to court and sued and filed two lawsuits, then you should have respectfully returned the Fadak. However, not returning the property of Amma Fatima was a big blunder of the Ummah.

"Dar e Zahra se lekar, Roza e Zahra giraane tak,
Ye ummat khud batati hai, Qayaamat kyun zaroori hai".

I also do not say that all the blame should be put on one person who is sitting on the throne and only he should be proved wrong because the fact is that from the people sitting in the government, to the advisors and to those who do not testify, even the spectators, everyone was wrong. It should have happened that the whole Ummah should have gathered at the door of Zahra Salamullah Alaiha and should have come forward in defense and protection of the daughter of Rasoolullah, but the vice versa happened and no one was there to raise their voice and apart from a few Sahabas, everyone left the Ahlebait of Rasool alone.

If you peep into the history, you will find that after the demise of Rasulullah, Fatima Salamullah Alaiha was the real heir of the Prophet and therefore she should have been consulted in every important matter. Her husband Maula Ali Alaihissalam, in that era was 'Waris-e-Dastar-e-Nabi', 'Wasi-e-Rasool', 'Babul Ilm', etc. so he too should have been consulted as well, but the Ummah not only took the decision of the Caliphate without the consultation of Fatima Salamullah Alaiha and Ali Alaihissalam but also snatched away the land of Fadak from her.

It is also true that Amma Fatima Salamullah Alaiha had no desire for wealth. But people could not understand Amma Fatima Salamullah Alaiha's repeated visits to the court after Fadak being snatched away, and a Pakistani terrorist, Mullah ji, associated with Dawat-e-Islami, which calls itself head of Barelvi Maslak, even dared to say that, "When the daughter of Rasool went to ask for Fadak, she was at fault.", Mazallah (God Forbid). The statement of this cursed one has forced that now things should be said openly, otherwise people used to remain silent earlier also because there is already a lot of difference of opinion on this matter and by talking about these historical things, this difference of opinions will increase and spread further.

If someone illegally occupies our land, is it a crime to ask for it back? If the government snatches away our father's inheritance, is it a crime to demad it back? The most important thing is that Fadak belonged to Fatima Salamullah Alaiha and Rasoolullah Sallallahu Alaihe Wa Aalihi Wa Sallam, had apparently given it to his daughter i.e. Fatima Salamullah Alaiha in his lifetime, before leaving this world for the heavenly abode. When it was snatched away, Amma Fatima asked for her right back. So demanding one's rights is also not wrong, raising voice if rights are snatched is also not wrong. It is also not wrong to make the government realize that governance without justice is valueless. It is also not at all wrong to become the first woman lawyer and advocate for the rights of all women.

However, the questions that arose after not giving Fadak are still enough to explain the difference between truth and falsehood. Amma Fatima Salamullah Alaiha may not have received Fadak, but she went to the court, spread the truth, and saved the 'Deen-e-Haq'. Every slave of Ahlebayt knows that, the one question of Fatima Salamullah Alaiha, and the arguments of the verses of the Qur'an given to prove her right and all the witnesses, sketches a distinct line between truth and falsehood. No one can pay the price for the favors that the daughter of Rasulullah has bestowed on us. She also saved the Haqiqi Deen and Haqiqi Shariah from being erased after the demise of Rasulullah and also blocked the ways of imposition of the orders of the government on the people instead of the commands of Allah and Rasulullah and thus she saved Islam, Quran, Shariat, Tawheed, Rasalat, Wilayat and Imamate even by giving her life. Allahu Akbar Kaseeran Kaseera. Allahumma Salle Ala Muhammad Wa Ala Aale Muhammad.

"Karam ka maksad, sakha ka markaz, Ata saraapa Janaab e Zahra, Nabi ki seerat, Nabi ki soorat, Nabi ka naqsha Janaab e Zahra".

I have already explained the issue of Bagh-e-Fadak in detail in my two books named "Shia-Sunni ....Ikhtilaf, galat fahmi aur Saazish" and "Do Islam... Haqiqi Islam aur Takhliki Islam mein fark". If my brothers and sisters want, they can also read these books. May Allah Rab ul Izzat make all of us the ones who hold the Quran and Ahlebait Alaihimussalam.

ﭘﭘﭘ

TWENTY-NINE
HAQQ E ALI

After the demise of Rasulullah, the Ummah should have come under the guardianship of their Maula but the opposite happened, people left Maula Ali Alaihissalam i.e. rejected the Caliph chosen by Allah and themselves elected the Caliph of their own choice and that too without consulting Maula Ali Alaihissalam. Later on his wife was oppressed and her Fadak was also snatched away and Ahl Bait e Rasool Alaihmussalam was left alone.

While returning from his last Hajj, at the place of Ghadir-e-Khum, Rasullulah Sallallahu Alaihe wa Aalihi Wasallam ordered everyone to stay, and even sent some people in both directions, so that those who have gone ahead or left behind can also be gathered at the place of Ghadir-e-Khum. The weather was extremely hot with hot sand that the pulpit was made on which the Beloved of Allah, Muhammad Sallallahu Alaihi Wa Aalihi Wasallam, delivered the sermon and in that speech, he clearly ordered to hold the Quran and Ahlebait and also stated that after him the Ummah should be kind towards his Ahlebait Alaihimussalam because he knew both the things by the order of God that after some time (months) he will not be present among the Ummah and that the Ummah will ill-treat Ahlebait Alaihimussalam. Rasoolullah, by the command of God, announced publicly "Man Kunto Maula Fa Hazaa Aliyun

Maula" i e "Whomever I am the Master, Ali is also his Master".
Allahumma Salle Ala Muhammad wa Ala Aale Muhammad.

It is even found in the history that there have been 1 lakh 24
thousand or about 2 lakh narrators of this hadith who themselves
heard this announcement, so it became impossible to falsify this
hadith, but still people who had gone crazy in jealousy started
messing up with it's meaning and thereby wrongly translated it and
said that Maula meant ' a friend' instead of 'a leader or Master'.The
first thing is that if you read the entire sermon and try to
understand it, you will find that in Ghadir, Rasulullah Sallallahu
Alaihe Wa Aalihi Wasallam had appointed his successor, i.e. 'Wasi
and Waris, a Dastaar' and infact announced the actual Caliph of
Allah's Caliphate.

The second thing is that if the illiterates are to be believed, then
according to them, Muhammad Rasulullah Sallallahu Alaihe Wa
Aalihi Wasallam stopped everyone at Ghadeer-e-Khum while
returning from the last Hajj. Those who went ahead, called them
back and those who were left behind, sent a message to them to
travel quickly and reach Ghadeer as soon as possible. Gathered
millions of Muslims and Companions. Under the hot sun, in the hot
sand, he made a pulpit and gave a sermon in front of millions of
people just to say that Ali Alaihissalam is your friend? i.e to establish
friendship? Only Allah can save the Ummah from the stupid talks
of these illiterates as they corrupt the faith and beliefs of common
people. May Allah curse the liars.

Maula Ali Alaihissalam is the actual successor of the Messenger of
Allah, whom the Ummah did not accept. Maula Ali Alaihissalam,
is the viceregent of the Prophet, whom the ummah did not believe.
Maula Ali Alaihissalaam, is the 'Wasi' of Muhammad Rasoolullah

Sallallahu Alaihe wa Aalihi Wasallam, whom the Ummah did not accept. Ali Alaihissalam, is the Maula, the Caliph of Allah, but the Ummah tried everything possible to keep him away from the Caliphate. He is the leader of the Imamate, but the Ummah did not accept his Imamate and He is only the leader of the Wilayat, in fact no Wali can be a Wali until Ali accepts the Wilayat of Ali.

First of all, people did not believe in Maula Ali Alaihissalam and those who believed, they did not believe in the way they were commanded to believe. Some believed it verbally and some believed merely for outward showoff while the truth is that the Caliphate, Wilayat and Imamate all were the rights of Maula Ali Alaihissalam, and it is still today. You might be surprised to know that there is only one Ameerul Momineen in this Ummah and that is Ali Alaihissalam. The matter of concern is that when Rasulullah Sallallahu Alaihe Wa Aalihi Wasallam was bodily alive, Maula Ali Alaihissalam was then also called Ameerul Momineen meaning that he is the Ameerul Momineen created by Allah and Rasoolullah.However, the cause of your surprise is that this Ummah has also called some other people as Ameerul Momineen. Now they are even trying to bless Abul Yazeed and Yazeed with this title. May Allah curse the liars.

The sad thing is that the Ummah has usurped each and every right of Maula Ali Alaihissalam and is still doing it today. In the earlier period, abuses and curses were hurled at Ali Alaihissalam from the pulpits, today the Marwanis do not have the courage to say anything bad about him openly, but their efforts are still in process, trying to reduce the virtues of Ali Alaihissalam, from the pulpits and spread the false praises of his enemies. However, it is impossible for creatures to reduce the glory of Ali whom Allah has made 'ALI'. Illa MaShaAllah.

Our Beloved Muhammad Sallallahu Alaihi wa Aalihi Wasallam himself said, "Ali is with the Haqq, the Haqq is with Ali.", "Ali is with the Quran, the Quran is with Ali". "I and Ali have been created from the same light (Noor) of God". "My flesh and Ali's flesh are one, my blood and Ali's blood are one.", "Ali is my guardian and brother in this world and the hereafter.","Ali is to me, like Haroon was to Moses", "Whose master I am, Ali is also their master.", "Ali is from me, I am from Ali.", "The best man of my Ummah is Ali.", "Ali is the root of faith.", "Ali is the father of wisdom.", "I am the city of knowledge and Ali is its gate.", "The leaders of the young men of Paradise are Hasan and Hussain and their father is even greater than them", Ali is the Wali of Allah", "Ali is the one who loves Allah and me the most and Allah and I love him the most.","No one knows Ali except me or the Lord", "If I had not been afraid that people would consider him as God like they did to Jesus, I would have told people more of Ali's virtues.", "Ali's will is my will." , "Ali is my soul.", "Ali is the servant of Allah.", "Ali is the one who sold his life for the will of God.", "Ali is my Aamil.", " Ali's zikr(chant and remembrance) is worship.", etc.

"Padhkar hadees e paak e Nabi ehsaas ye hua,
Ki Ahmad ki baaton-baaton mein, Haidar ki baat hai"

Allahumma Salle Ala Muhammad wa Ala Aale Muhammad.

In the books of both Shia and Sunni schools, there are maximum numbers of hadiths in the glory of Maula Ali Alaihissalam. But the sad thing is that even after listening to so many hadiths of the Holy Prophet Sallalahu Alaihi Wa Aalihi Wasallam, the Muslim could not understand the truth or perhaps he was so blinded by the worldly desires that he made Yazid's forefathers as patrons because it is unimaginable to be able to commit evil while living under the patronage of Maula Ali Alaihissalam.

The biggest difficulty in supporting Maula Ali Alaihissalam was that the worldly people had to leave behind greed, envy, promiscuity,evil, adultery,and all such sins and wicked deeds and follow Deen-e-Islam and follow the true religion and the true Shariat and at every step one had to fulfill the commands of Allah and his Prophet . To follow the path of Maula Ali Alaihissalam meant to observe the deen, which was not easy at all for those who considered Islam as a rule or government. All the people, who are fond of creating Takhliqi (made up) Deen and Takhliqi (fake) Shariat, stood against Maula Ali Alaihissalam.

The Companions who supported Maula Ali Alaihissalam were very few and the Sahaba who supported Ali Alaihissalam were killed just because of their love and support towards Ali Alaihissalam. This kind of events which started with the demise of Rasulullah, gradually increased and did not stop even after the demise and martyrdom of Maula Ali i.e., hundreds of Sahabas and Tabaeen were killed, for example Hazrat Owais Karni, Hazrat Meesam e Tammar, Hazrat Hujr bin Adi etc.

It is surprising that Ali, for whom Rasulullah Sallallahu Alaihi wa Aalihi Wasallam had said, "Ali is with Haqq, Haqq is with Ali", the Muslims themselves fought with him and the height was that Amma Ayesha Radiyallahu Anha was also provoked and brought to the battlefield to fight with Ali Alaihissalam. It is the grace of Allah that Maula Ali Alaihissalam received the apparent caliphate and it was received within 30 years of the demise of Rasulullah otherwise the clerics would have made immense void efforts to stop his mentions and disregard his virtues and also distance people from Ahlebait Alaihimusallam.

If Maula Ali wouldn't have got this caliphate, then this Maulvi would start calling him even lower than the fourth, but anyways the name and grace of one whom has Allah elevated, the Maulvi can never stop his praises even if he wants to. Illa Masha'Allah.

You can find by reading Islamic history that after the demise of Rasulullah, Maula Ali Alaihissalam chose to remain silent and secluded, he did not take part in any war or jihad, although whenever any Caliph faced difficulties or could not answer, they came to Ali Alaihissalam for help and he always helped them but kept himself away from politics, caliphate, and government, and when he got the apparent caliphate, he also waged war and jihad and tried to remove the misconception and altered traditions made during the earlier period.

"Bas sukoot hai kamre mein,
Khaamoshiyaan pinha hain
Sau raaz keh rahi hain,
Aye Ali! teri tanhaiyan."

So my loved ones! Maula Ali Alaihissalam's rights were usurped in every era and he was persecuted a lot. Atrocities were perpetrated on his children in every era and those atrocities are continuing till date. I have read the books of history and did not find anyone more oppressed than the Ahlebait Alaihimussalam. May Allah Rab ul Izzat make us all believers of Tawheed, Risalat as well as Wilayat-e-Ali Alaihissalam, followers of Aiyimma e Ahlebait Alaihimussalam and steadfast holders of Quran and Ahlebait Alaihimussalam.

If you want to read about Maula Ali Alaihissalam's Caliphate, Wilayat, Imamat, knowledge, battles etc., then you can read another book written by me "Wasi-e-Rasool". In that book, I have tried to explain these big issues precisely and in simple language so that even our youth who do not like to read much can read and understand easily. Allahu Akbar Kaseeran Kaseera. Allahumma Salle Ala Muhammad wa Ala Aale Muhammad.

ᛞᛞᛞ

THIRTY
HAQQ E HASAN

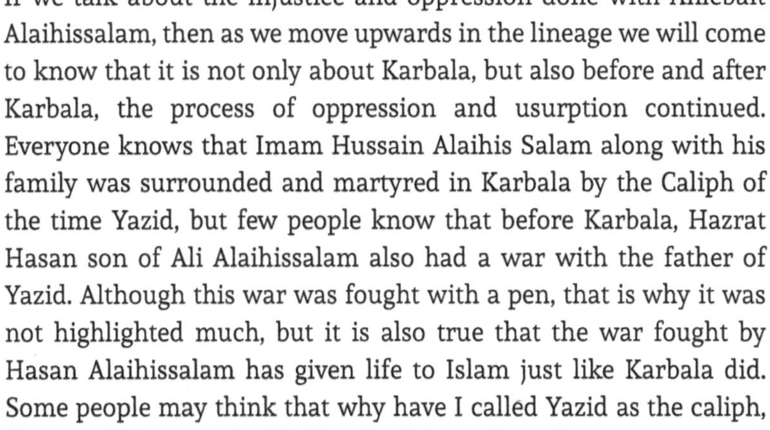

If we talk about the injustice and oppression done with Ahlebait Alaihissalam, then as we move upwards in the lineage we will come to know that it is not only about Karbala, but also before and after Karbala, the process of oppression and usurption continued. Everyone knows that Imam Hussain Alaihis Salam along with his family was surrounded and martyred in Karbala by the Caliph of the time Yazid, but few people know that before Karbala, Hazrat Hasan son of Ali Alaihissalam also had a war with the father of Yazid. Although this war was fought with a pen, that is why it was not highlighted much, but it is also true that the war fought by Hasan Alaihissalam has given life to Islam just like Karbala did. Some people may think that why have I called Yazid as the caliph, then my dear ones, the Muslims had themselves chosen an accursed like Yazid bin Muawiyah as the seventh caliph of Islam, I may not like him, but the Muslims of that time had paid allegiance to him only.

After Maula Ali Alaihissalam, Imam Hasan Alaihissalam got the Caliphate, but Muawiya created an atmosphere against him and started preparing to fight against him. Imam Hasan Alaihissalam never wanted to fight over trivial things like governance and did not want mass killings to take place, so he tried to avoid the war like situations. When Muawiya asked him to leave the Caliphate, Imam Hasan Alaihissalam reconciled with him and left the caliphate peacefully and quietly started spreading the true religion. It should also be remembered here that Imam Hasan Alaihissalam had reconciled on his own terms and had cut off the tongue of the enemies of Islam with his pen itself. In my previous book, "Shia-Sunni.... Ikhtilaf, Ghalat-Fahmi aur Saazish", I have tried to explain Sulah-e-Imam Hasan Alaihissalam (Reconciliation of Imam Hasan Alaihissalam) in detail. You can also read that book if you want.

"Hasan wo hain ki jinse duniya ne deen liya,
Wo jinke naam se bakhshish ka bhi yaqeen liya,
Ali ke laadle bete ne Shaam walon se,
Qalam ki nok pe lafz e Ameer chheen liya."

However, the reality is that when Imam Hasan Alaihissalam was doing the Caliphate, then the right of the Caliphate was taken away from him and Abul Yazid converted the Caliphate into a complete rule. Although earlier also the Caliphate was bent on being converted into a government, but Abul Yazid completed the rest of the work. Later, the Peace Treaty that he had signed with Hasan Alaihissalam was also broken and in this way his right was usurped again.

Although Imam Hasan Alaihissalam never had any interest in Caliphate because he always wanted to serve and spread the true religion, but still he always kept stinging in the eyes of the government and finally the government got him poisoned and martyred him. This oppression itself was not less but in addition to it, his body was bled to death by shooting arrows at them at his funeral and he was not even allowed to be buried near his maternal grandfather Muhammad Sallallahu Alaihe wa Aalihi Wasallam. It is also an oppression of the Ummah that the Ahlebait of Rasulullah was not allowed to be buried near Rasulullah Sallallahu Alaihe wa Aalihi Wasallam. Later the Muslims broke the tomb of Hasan Alaihissalam and expressed their anger and hatred.

"Kiya Qasim ne hamla baad mein, pehle ye farmaya,
Main wo hoon jiske baba ka kalam, talwaar jaisa hai,
Nikalta hai to har dushman ka seena cheer deta hai,
Mere baba ka qalam, Dada ki Zulfiqaar jaisa hai".

If we think carefully, we will find that the foundation of the Battle of Karbala was laid in Badr itself, the situation was worse during the time of Imam Hasan Alaihissalam, it seemed that the true Islam would be completely destroyed and the artificial (made up) Islam would be imposed on the people but Hazrat Hasan Alaihissalam understood the delicacy of time and situation and took the right decision at the right time and took the time to spread the true Deen (religion). During this, he taught hundreds of Saadats and non Saadats, the knowledge of true religion and Shariat and sent them out of Arabia to every corner of the world so that true religion could remain safe. Imam Hasan Alaihissalam's hard work was done with silence, so only the Ahle Zarf (Noble men) could understand it's value.

"Hussain Qaid e Azam hai Haqparaston ka,
Jo maanta nahi hai shaks, dil ka khota hai,
Hussain saare zamaane se badh gaya lekin,
Kiya jo gaur to dekha, Hasan se chhota hai".

ﭑﭑﭑ

THIRTY-ONE
HAQQ E HUSSAIN

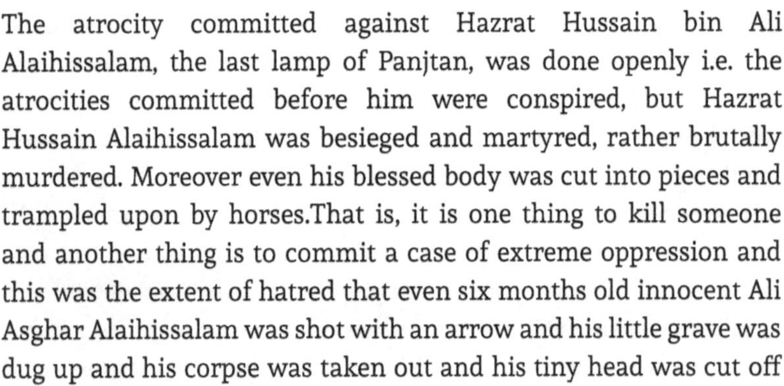

The atrocity committed against Hazrat Hussain bin Ali Alaihissalam, the last lamp of Panjtan, was done openly i.e. the atrocities committed before him were conspired, but Hazrat Hussain Alaihissalam was besieged and martyred, rather brutally murdered. Moreover even his blessed body was cut into pieces and trampled upon by horses.That is, it is one thing to kill someone and another thing is to commit a case of extreme oppression and this was the extent of hatred that even six months old innocent Ali Asghar Alaihissalam was shot with an arrow and his little grave was dug up and his corpse was taken out and his tiny head was cut off and raised on a spear.

So, the Ummah has usurped his rights since he was young, but this process did not stop. According to the Peace Treaty of Hasan Alaihissalam, after Muawiya, the caliphate should have been given to Hussain Alaihissalam but Muawiya broke the covenant and placed a caliph like accursed Yazid on the head of the Ummah.

They tried to force allegiance from Hussain Alaihissalam, but he refused to give it and finally he was surrounded. When there was no way left for peace and neither he was allowed to go from there,Imam Hussain Alaihissalam chose the path of Jihad and sacrificed everything for the sake of Allah and eventually became a martyr himself.

Yazidi-Marwani clerics falsely accuse you that you went to fight Yazid for the Caliphate, although this accusation is false and baseless. Yes, you wanted to help the Kufis and destroy the Takhliqi Deen created by Yazid, just like Imam Hasan Alaihissalam did, but now the question had changed. Now, the demand was for allegiance and not the Caliphate and It is not permissible even for a common Muslim to pledge allegiance to an oppressor, then he is 'Sibt e Rasool'. He thus refused and by giving the blood of his family in Karbala, by giving his blood he revived Islam.

"Jab bhi kabhi zameer ka sauda ho doston,
Qaayam raho Hussain ke inkar ki tarah..."

In fact, I wrote the book "Shia-Sunni...Ikhtilaf,Galatfahmi aur Saazish" to try to fill the gap between Shias and Sunnis, but it also includes the issues related to Imam Hussain and Karbala which are the reason for the differences between Shia-Sunni. Although there has never been a difference between Shia-Sunni, if we remove the imposed fake religion of Maulvis-Zakirs and return to the real religion. Anyways if you wish, you can read many things related to Karbala, Muharram, Imam Hussain Alaihissalam in detail in that book. In this book, I am talking about the rights of Hussain. So my loved ones! The Ummah was supposed to treat the leader of the youth of Paradise with kindness and consider him as their Imam and follow him, but on the contrary the Ummah itself became thirsty for his blood.

Some people think that after the incident of Karbala the situation would have improved, but it was not. The children of Hasnain Karimain Alaihimusallam were hunted down and killed in every era, infact our Aiyamma e Ahlebayt Alaihimusallam was also martyred by giving poison, i.e. the descendants of Imam Hasan Alaihissalam and Imam Hussain Alaihissalam or I can say that an attempt was made to destroy the family of Muhammad Rasoolullah Sallallahu Alaihi wa Aalihi Wasallam, although it was not in their power to do so, because these devils can never end the progeny of that family whose last Imam is protected by Allah Himself? Supporting whom was obligatory on the ummah, the ummah martyred them in a state of thirst and killed their children, family members and slaves.

"Qatl e Hussain asl mein marg e yazeed hai
Islam zinda hota hai, Har Karbala ke baad".

All the Saadat and all the slaves of Ahlebait Alaihimussalam! The time is near when this ummah will declare us as impudent of Companions of Rasulullah and issue a fatwa of justified murder for us. The reason would be that you and I believe in the Companions like Hazrat Salman, Hazrat Abuzar, Hazrat Miqdad, Hazrat Malik, Hazrat Habib, Hazrat Bilal, Hazrat Ammar, but don't believe in the favourite Companions as declared by the clerics like Muawiya, Marwan, Mugira etc. Although the love and support of Sahaba is not even made obligatory on the Ummah, but still we believe and sacrifice our lives in the footsteps of those Sahaba who were loyal with Ahlebait Alaihimussalam.

Even Janab-e-Fizza, who was the servant of Amma Fatima Salamullah Alaiha, is also called Amma Fizza by us. Hazrat Qambar, who was the slave of Maula Ali Alaihissalam, is also revered by us.

The extent of our love and respect is that we even respect the horse of Ameerul Momineen Maula Ali Alaihissalam and Imam Hussain Alaihissalam. We even respect a sword like Zulfikar, so how is it possible that we would not respect the Companions. So my loved ones! Forgetting the purpose of Hussain Alaihissalam is also the violation of rights of Imam Hussain. We need to remember the purpose of Imam Hussain Alaihissalam and keep trying to spread his purpose and message.

In the end, I will just say that Imam-e-Qayyim, Imam Mehdi Alaihissalam is also an offspring of Imam e Hussain Alaihissalam and all the lovers of Imam Hussain should become Imam Mehdi's helpers and supporters. First of all the Sadaats should come forward and try to start preparations for Imam's army. We need to search for diamonds like John and invite people like Hurr. The door of Ahlebait is open to all and Saadats should not forget the purpose of their ancestors.May Allah Rabb ul Izzat make us all follow the right religion and enable us to help Imam-e-Qayyam. My loved ones! Do spread Karbala. Allahu Akbar Kaseeran Kaseera. Allahumma Salle Ala Muhammad wa Ala Aale Muhammad.

"Zarb Haidar ke sar par ya Hasan ko zeher dena,
Karbala jal jal ke kehti hai, adal zaruri hai,
Qatl e Zahra se lekar, Mazar e Zahra giraane tak,
Ye ummat khud batati hai, Qayamat kyun zaruri hai"

৩৩৩

THIRTY-TWO
TWO NOOSES

My dear ones! No matter how much Yazidi and Marwani clerics try, there are two such nooses around their necks because of which their hypocrisy comes out. One is Bagh e Fadak and the other is Imaan e Abu Talib. Even though the Yazidi cleric does not love Ahlebait Alaihimusallam, but he also has to make a claim of love for them because despite adding the descriptions of the Sahaba in the Durood o Salawat, the cleric could not enter the names of Sahaba in the Durud that is recited in the Namaz. Some clerics even accept that Abul Yazid was wrong to prove their love, but when it comes to the issue of the land of Fadak, their tongues also gets twisted. We don't have any problem with anyone, whether he is of this era or of the previous era, whether people call him Sahaba or Khalifa or Governor or Tabaeen or Wali. But whenever the matter of Fadak will be raised, the truth will always be said and the truth is that snatching Fadak from Amma Fatimah Salamullah Alaiha is one of the biggest blunders of the Ummah. In this book only I have written a topic called "Haqq-e-Fatima", in which I have written about Bagh-e-Fadak and you may have read it.

"Sawaal kar chuki Zahra, Jawaab lena hai,
Fadak ka Mehdi ko aakar, Hisaab lena hai"

There is another noose around Maulvi's neck and that is Imaan e Abu Talib ,i.e, the faith of Abu Talib. Since they envy Maula Ali Alaihissalam, therefore these 'Mulla ji' try very hard to prove his father an infidel or Kafir. In our belief, Sarkar Abu Talib is not only a Muslim, a believer, but his status is much higher than that of the Sahabas. He defended and protected Muhammad Sallallahu Alaihe Wa Aalihi Wa Sallam and stood as a shield to protect the Deen-e-Haq. The one whom the enemies of the religion, the enemies of Rasoolullah, feared was only Hazrat Abu Talib.

This is also an oppression of the clerics that, the one who spent his entire life in the protection of Islam and Rasoolullah Sallallahu Alaihi Wa Aalihi Wa Sallam was declared Kafir and the one who abused Rasoolullah throughout his life, pelted stones at him, he was declared Sahaba and his children were also declared Sahaba. May Allah curse the liars. Allahu Akbar Kaseeran Kaseera.

Sarkar Abu Talib recited these verses while describing the glory of Allah Rabb ul Izzat -

مليك الناس ليس له شيريك

هو الوهاب والمبدى المعيد

ومن تحت الشماء بحق

ومن فوق الشماء له عبيد

"Allah is the Lord of every creature. He has power over everything and He has no partner.
It is Allah who showers His mercy on everyone, it is Allah who created the entire universe. He is the one who made man alive while he was dead.

Every life that is between Paradise and the world and those above Paradise and beyond it whatever has been created is created by only one Lord."

Now think yourself, can a person who recites such beautiful verses in the glory of Allah Rabb ul Izzat be a disbeliever?, In order to read and understand more you can read another book of mine, written in Hindi, named "Diwan e Abu Talib" which is a collection of more than 60 poems written by Sarkar Hazrat Abu Talib. In this book, Hazrat Abu Talib is introduced and I have tried to explain his life as well. Hazrat Abu Talib's hard work for the protection of Rasulullah Sallallahu Alaihi wa Aalihi Wasallam has been described and how Hazrat Abu Talib fought against the enemy's conspiracies against Deen and how he saved Islam has also been described in the book.

"Puchhte ho humse 'Syed', Unke imaan ki daleel
Rab e kaaba ki kasam, khud Rab Abu Talib ka hai "
    "Ban gaya Noor e Khuda, Deen e Nabi ki dhaal bhi,
Arey! Har Sahaba se bada, Imaan Abu Talib ka hai".

ﯕﯕﯕ

THIRTY-THREE

'SULAH-E-HASAN AND 'JUNG-E-HUSSAIN'

A Maulvi Sahab began to spread this fitna that "We cannot fight with the one with whom Hazrat Hasan made peace and we cannot make peace with the one with whom Hazrat Hussain fought a war." The surprising thing is that such childish statements, are coming out from the side of famous Maulvi Hazrat and it is a matter of shame that that Maulvi Sahib himself is a 'Saadat'. Sometimes ago, this same cleric had called Hazrat Abu Talib a Kafir, although later he had repented and corrected himself but people should understand that the way his belief on Hazrat Abu Talib Alaihissalam was wrong and later after investigation, he rectified it. Similarly his beliefs on Sulah-e-Hasan (Peace treaty of Hasan) and Jung-e-Hussain (War of Hussain) may also be wrong. We hope that by the grace of God this cleric will definitely rectify this belief too after further investigation. Illa Masha'Allah.

Another Maulvi Sahab even crossed all limits and went so far as to say, "Hazrat Hasan was mild-tempered, so he reconciled, while Hazrat Hussain was short tempered, so he fought." Now Allah knows better how do these clerics even speak such childish meaningless things and why?

I would like to answer all these fitnas spread by these clerics. The first thing is that when does the situation require reconciliation? It is obvious that whenever there is a situation for war, there is either war or mutual reconciliation. It was Abul Yazid's mistake in trying to clash with Sibt e Rasool. However, Maulvi Sahib presents it as if Abul Yazid was a very virtuous and good man. They say if he would have been bad, why would the Imam reconcile with him? My loved ones! Ask the clerics, who is reconciled with? Is there never any reconciliation done with the enemies ?

If reconciliation of Hasan Alaihissalam means that the opposition was right, then Hasan alaihissalam's maternal grandfather, Muhammad Sallallahu Alaihe wa Alihi Wasallam is superior to him. He himself reconciled with the Kuffar in Makkah, which is known as the 'Sulah e Hudaibiya'. So what will you say about this now? The Kuffars of Makkah were noble and honorable, so Rasulullah himself reconciled with them?, MazAllah.

When the Meccan Kuffars (blasphemers) broke the terms of peace, then Rasool-e-Khuda Muhammad Sallallahu Alaihe Wa Alihi Wasallam himself even fought with them. That is, it has been proven that reconciliation is a sign for enmity and the opposition can be bad, infact most of the time, situation of reconciliation comes only when one is right and the other is wrong, and when it comes to Ahlebayt, everything becomes crystal clear, who is with the truth and who is wrong?

Now it is also important to see how many conditions of Sulah-e-Hasan did Abul Yazid fulfill and if he broke the conditions, then this is also a big blunderer in itself because a Muslim does not break the contract made with another Muslim, rather a Muslim does not break a contract with anyone. He also fulfills the promises made to humans and other creatures. Now that Abul Yazid had not fulfilled the terms of reconciliation and had broken all the terms, war was bound to happen anyway; although Ahlebait Alaihissalam tried their best to prevent it so that the lives and property of other innocent people would be spared and they are not harmed. Because war gives nothing but loss.

Imam Hasan Alaihissalam saved millions of people from dying by reconciliation and protected humanity. At the same time, he sought respite by reconciling, in which he also worked to save the true Islam and give people the right training. It is also true that at least 72 faithful were there in Karbala, but in the circumstances when Imam Hasan reconciled, it was difficult to find even this number of people because the people of that period had either given allegiance to the enemy out of fear of the government or some had sold their conscience.

Anyways! Hazrat Hasan Alaihissalam was martyred by poisoning. It is also true that Imam Hasan Alaihissalam was martyred before the Battle of Karbala, but Hazrat Qasim's war with the son of Muawiya in the Battle of Karbala is a clear proof that if Hazrat Hasan Alaihissalam would have been mortally present during the Battle, he would have fought this great war and as the Imam and Sardar of Ahlebait Alaihimusallam and all slaves and followers of Ahlebayt would have been their leader and guardian and tried to keep them safe in his shadow.

"Imaam Hasan ki fazilat nahin samjhi ye duniya
Aapki shaan ye hai aap, Hussain ke bhi Imaam hain".

"Salaam ho Muhammad o Aal e Muhammad par,
Salaam ho ajdaad e Muhammad par,
Salaam ho aulaad e Muhammad par,
Salaam ho Karbala mein shaheed hone wale har ek shohda par,
Salaam ho Mohsin e Islaam, Hasnain Karimain ke dada, **Hazrat Abu Talib** par.
    Allahumma Salle Ala Muhammad wa Ala Aale Muhammad."

Now we might have understood Sulh-e-Hasan Alaihissalam, but by giving an example, I would like to explain Sulh-e-Hasan and Jung-e-Hussain in an easier way. I like to explain by giving examples because even Allah likes this way of explaining things.

"Zaruri nahin har kaam Zulfiqar se hi ho,
Kalam se fatah karna koi Imaam se seekhe".

My dear people! Let me give you an example, once upon a time there was a person who got an injury in his leg, he went to the doctor prescribed medicine but that person did not take the medicine. The disease continued to increase, now that person was negligent, he neither took medicine nor any precautions, then he went to another doctor and he said that your leg will have to be amputated? What does this mean? Was one doctor right and the other wrong? No. Rather, the disease itself is now different, so the treatment has to be different.

The surprising thing is that even the people who are known as high profiled ulemas also tell lies to prove their sect because I can't believe that they don't even have the basic knowledge of the era of Hasan Alaihissalam and that of Hussain Alaihissalam. It is not so that they are unaware of the changing circumstances of that period, but all these seditions and mischiefs are deliberately raised in order to create discord among the people and extort funds in the name of sect. Actually, what according to the Maulvi is one issue are actually two different issues.

Abul Yazid had asked Hazrat Hasan Alaihissalam for caliphate. That is, he was ready to fight considering caliphate as the ultimate government and rule and thus he was determined to kill innocent Muslims in the greed of the throne. At that time Hazrat Hasan Alaihissalam made peace with him in order to save millions of Muslims and Deen-e-Haqq (The True Religion).

Yazid had asked Hazrat Hussain Alaihissalam for 'Baiyat' (Oath of Allegiance) and Imam Hussain Alaihissalam did not give 'Baiyat' to that wretched person and it is not the practice of Ahlebait Alaihimusallam that they would give Baiyat to Yazid or anyone else while being the master themselves. The Imam tried his best to avoid the war, but when the Yazidi army surrounded the house of Muhammad Rasulullah, Imam Hussain Alaihissalam chose the path of 'Jihad for the sake of Allah' and saved 'Haqq Deen' by sacrificing his family.

What 'Maulvi Sahab' is unable to understand is that if Abul Yazid had asked Imam Hasan Alaihissalam for the pledge of allegiance, a war like Karbala would have taken place only at that time, and if Yazid had asked for Caliphate solely instead of the pledge of allegiance, Imam Hussain would have given it without any second thought just like his brother and Imam, Hasan Alaihissalam, had given it, i.e. by reconciliation.

"Faisle kaise lete hain, Fatima ke laal se seekho
Kahaan par sulah hoti hai, Kahaan par jung karni hai".

I also understand the helplessness of Marwani clerics. In the name of opposition to Ahle Tashayyo, wrong beliefs are being planted in the hearts and minds of the youth of their respective sects and they are being trapped in the net by making fake talks. You may also be wondering why I repeatedly say that Yazidi clerics have spread this communal riots for charity. You might think that the difference of beliefs is the main reason for the distance, but in reality there are only two important and real issues of difference, the first is donation, the cleric of every sect wants to get maximum donations, the more Muslims join them, the more donation they will be able to collect. The second reason is to impose their Maulvi, their ideology and books written on others and prove themselves as promoters and contractors of religion.

My loved ones! Seeking knowledge and researching in the light of Quran and Ahlebayt is the only way through which you can reach the truth. Knowledge is necessary to attain 'Marifat' and to get knowledge and guidance, it is necessary that you should be the one who firmly holds the Quran and Ahlebait Alaihissalam. Your clerics never want you to gain knowledge and research, so they try to limit you to only one sect and its books.

"Khulta hai ye raaz bhi taleem o tahqeeq ke baad,
Deen e Haq, imaan hai aur Deen e mulla, kufr hai".

With full honesty, taking off the glasses of sects, get knowledge with full justice, read the authors of different sects too, see who has wanted to tell what?,How much is it right?, how much is wrong? Try to understand, investigate and contemplate then you will find the truth automatically.
In Sha Allah. Allahu Akbar Kaseeran Kaseera. Allahumma Salle Ala Muhammad wa Ala Aale Muhammad.

ԵԵԵ

THIRTY-FOUR

Hal Min Nasirin Yansurna

Maula Hussain Alaihissalam was calling for help at the time of 'Asr-i-Ashura'. Imagine this situation in this way that an old father is present in the house, if his house is attacked and the attackers kill all the members of his household, then will that old father also prefer to die or live?, Think about the answer yourself. Now, such would be the situation of a common man, now lets talk about 'Sibt e Rasool'. Hussain Alaihissalam, have picked up and buried the corpses of his sons, brothers, nephews, lovers, slaves, and the time of Asr has come, and Imam Hussain Alaihissalam is calling for help and saying in a loud voice, "Hal min Nasirin Yansurna.", Why? To save his life?

Hearing the call of Hazrat Hussain Alaihissalam, the angels and jinn came running, but Hussain Alaihissalam sent them back because the call of Hussain Alaihissalam was for humans. He, Hussain son of Ali Alaihissalam, for whom death was never an issue, that Hussain bin Ali Alaihissalam who had no fear except the fear of God, when he himself is calling for help, people should have understood that the call for help was made not to save his life but to for a specific cause, to save a specific purpose.

Every day is Karbala, every day is Ashura, every day the call of Hazrat Hussain Alaihissalam is echoing in the air, "Hal min Nasirin Yansurana?" My dear ones do remember, helping Imam e Qayam means helping Imam Hussain, and helping Imam Hussain means the help of Panjatan or Ahlebait, the help of Panjatan means the help of Deen and the help of Deen means helping Allah. Remember here, the meaning of the help of Hussain Alaihissalam is that we become the ones who spread the message and purpose of Hussain, the ones who has courage to call a spade, a spade that is clearly speaking the truth and rejecting the false. Hussain's help means help to spread the truth, help to expose Takhliqi Deen and help to revive Haqiqi Deen.

If you are truly loyal to Muhammad and his progeny, Aal e Muhammad, then your wish should to be to get a chance to sacrifice your lives for the purpose of Hussain Alaihissalaam. We should prepare for the arrival of Imam e Qaayam and fight every blow of the devil (Shaytaan). Calling the people towards goodness and truth and preventing them from going to evil and falsehood is the answer to the call of Hussain Alaihissalam.Tawheed, Risalat, Imamate, Wilayat, Deen-e-Islam, Quran, coming forward for the defense of humanity is the answer to Hussain Alaihissalam's call. Just raising slogans will not work, we have to sacrifice our lives, property, and time in real life at the ground level in order to save and spread 'Maqsad-e-Imam' (the pupose of Imam).

All Saadat and lovers of Ahlebayt should come out of sectarianism and leave their respective sects whose status is nothing compared to Deen-e-Haqq (The True Religion Islam), and try to eliminate the difference between Shia-Sunni, and come to the side of truth by leaving falsehood. Put an end to mutual enmity and gather at one gate i.e. Door of Ahlebait Alaihimusallam. Whether you are a Shia or a Sunni, Maulvis and Zakirs can do you no good, clinging to the Quran and Ahlebait Alaihimusallam is the only way to Allah. Allahu Akbar Kaseeran Kaseera. Allahumma Salle Ala Muhammad wa Ala Aale Muhammad.

"Momin aaj bhi Deen ast Hussain ko thaame hain
Jo raah bhatkati ho wo raah hargiz nahin chunte
Hal min ki sada dete hain Hussain aaj bhi
Gaflat mein pade log par ab bhi nahin sunte".

❦❦❦

THIRTY-FIVE
NUSRAT OF IMAM MAHDI

In the present times, to answer the call of Imam Hussain Alaihissalam, "Hal Min Nasirin Yansurna", it is necessary that we strive for the help and support of Imam e Qayam, who are among the sons of Imam Hussain, who is in concealment and will appear soon by God's command. He will fill the world with justice and fairness. Takhliqi (false and made up) Deen and Shariat will end and Haqiqi (Real) Deen and Shariat will be alive again. At that time, all these sects will disappear, the majority of the Ummah will die due to diseases and wars, and the remaining Ummah will be narrowed down and divided into only two parts, Lashkar-e-Mahdi (the army of Mahdi)which will be on the right side and Sufiani Lashkar (the army of Sufiyan)which will be on the wrong side.

Whenever we talk about Nusrat-e-Imam (Supporting the Imam), people often start saying, we dont have that much strength, we are poor, what can we do, etc. Supporting the Imam does not mean that you have to come out today and spend all your wealth or start a war with someone. Rather, we have to work hard for the appearance of Imam. Let me explain with an example, until we transform ourselves into the army of true religion, why and how will our

Imam reach us? When we ourselves are not ready for the reappearance of Imam-e-Qayyam, why will he reappear?,Nevertheless,Allah can send His Qayyam Imam whenever He wants.

"Muntazir ho agar Imaam Mahdi ke zuhoor ke
Nusrat Imaam e Qaayam ki tum bhi kiya karo."

So my loved ones! In order to help the Imam, first of all, it is important that we work hard on ourselves, that is, transform ourselves into a good person, a perfect Muslim, and a perfect believer. Try to improve your morals, your habits, your manners, behavior and your way of living. Try to get proper education and training. Strive to seek the knowledge of success in this world and the Hereafter and try to make yourself able to stay strong in this world as well.

After this, we should pay attention to our wife and our children, try to give them proper education and training. Give your children religious as well as worldly education. As I have said earlier in this book that when Imam e Qayam will appear and he will stay here, along with pious, religious, sincere,devout and dedicated people in his army, he will also need people having worldly knowledge and skills like scientists,researchers, doctors,engineers, teachers, professors, businessmen, entrepreneurs, lawyers, mechanics, computer operators, ethical hackers etc. too. Supporting Imam Alaihissalam does not only mean that one acquires religious knowledge and remains weak in worldly affairs. How much better it would be when we would have people who are also skilled in worldly education and art and are also religious.

When we reform ourselves and our wives and children, and start improving our practices, then we will have to strive to reform the rest of our household, family members, and relatives. Convey the true religion to them and keep trying to make them virtuous and honourable.Any change or improvement starts with oneself and then gradually this change spreads and takes the form of a revolution, when the revolution soares high, then the whole society, the whole country and even the whole world will perceive this change and improvement and will be impressed/affected by it.

So my dear ones! When we have worked on self improvement and that of our wife and children, then we need to extend this effort to our other family members, relatives, and after that we should reach out to our neighbours and the surrounding society. For this, it is important that we try to remove the evils and vices spread in the society. Try to clean the filth of our society and make efforts to connect people to the truth. For this, the most important thing is that we invite people towards 'Deen-e-Haqq' not only with our words but also with our actions.

Attention should be paid to the education of children, such madrasas should be built in which religious as well as worldly education is given, dowry system should be banned, extravagant spending should be stopped, unnecessary rituals should be prohibited,Nikah should be made easy and full of simplicity, pretense should stop. Veil and Sunnah should be made common. Ethics, education, training, behavior, manners, lifestyle should be improvised. Relatives-neighbors should be treated well. Violation and usurping of rights should end and one should continue to pay 'Huqooq ul Allah' and 'Huqooq ul Ibad'. Efforts should also be made to remove the fear of death from the hearts and to inculcate the spirit of martyrdom. That is, true religion should be made common and we should try to do everything that Allah, Rasoolullah and

'Aiyamma e Ahlebayt' and the Quran have commanded and taught and avoid everything that has been forbidden.

"Sipaahi banke pehle tum, Taiyaar karo khud ko
Jab lashkar taiyaar ho, Tab hi Salaar aata hai".

Saving people from falsehood, taking them towards truth. Supporting the oppressed, fighting the oppressor, spreading the difference between Halal and Haram, truth and falsehood, Calling people towards good deeds and stopping them from bad deeds is the way to 'Nusrat e Imam' that is, to support Imam e Qaayam. My loved ones! Keep trying to call the whole humanity towards Quran and Ahlebait Alaihimussalam. Keep spreading the message of Karbala . Allahu Akbar Kaseeran Kaseera.

ᗐᗐᗐ

Thank You

All opinions and advice in this book are solely those of the author, based on the teachings of Ahlulbayt Alaihimussalam. Care has been taken to ensure that the information in this book is true and correct. Any grammatical errors, typing mistakes or spelling errors are purely unintended.

The author expresses heartfelt gratitude to the readers for their love and support for the content and encourages them to conduct further research and strive to follow the straight path as responsible lovers of Ahlebayt Alaihimussalam.

This Ummah deviated from the Haq Deen (the straight path) soon after the demise of Rasulullah Sallallahu Alaihe Wa Ala Aalihi Wa Sallam, becoming followers of Takhliqi Deen. From Imam Ali Alaihissalam to Imam Hasan Askari Alaihissalam, every Imam of Ahl al-Bayt sought to uphold Haqiqi Deen in the face of Takhliqi Deen. Imam Mehdi Alaihissalam will also reappear to raise the flag of Haqiqi Deen.

Fatima Salamullah Alaiha was the first to rise against Takhliqi Deen in order to preserve the Deen of Allah. Imam Ali, Imam Hasan, and the entire progeny of Ahl al-Bayt Alaihimussalam were martyred in this struggle.

I have written this book with the intention of awakening people to understand the significance of Karbala and the motive of Imam Hussain Alaihissalam, urging them to strive to revive Haqiqi Deen. Our sole aim should be to live and die in support of Imam al-

Qayam.

Allahumma Salle Ala Muhammad wa Ala Aale Muhammad.

Assalam O Alaikum Wa Rahmatullahe Wa Barakatahu

ﻉﻉﻉ

www.ingramcontent.com/pod-product-compliance
Lightning Source LLC
Chambersburg PA
CBHW021203130726
47988CB00002B/487